Dispatches: T
in Theology and Global Crises

Dispatches draws on the legacy of early twentieth-century theological responses to the crises of the two world wars. During World War II, the *Signposts* (Dacre Press, 1940) series sought to offer an interruption of a theological malaise in the midst of mass violence and destruction. Contributors from that series, including Julian Casserly, Eric Mascall, and Donald MacKinnon, among others, offered slim volumes that drew from diverse resources and harnessed the apocalyptic political urgency of the dialectical school within the theological grammar of a more traditional Anglo-Catholic Thomism. Similarly, and inspired significantly by MacKinnon's contributions, this present series draws on diverse theological resources in order to offer urgent responses to contemporary crises.

While the title of the series conveys the digest nature of the volumes, the subtitle, *Turning Points*, indicates the apocalyptic urgency of the issues addressed. Yet, there is no prescriptive theological stream within which the tradition is to be reappropriated by our authors. The goal of the series is to offer a genuinely creative and disruptive theological-ethical *ressourcement* for church in the present moment. With conceptual agility and faithfulness this series will provide intelligent and yet accessible reflections on the shape and form of theological life in the present.

Dispatches will illuminate and explore, creatively and concisely, the implications and relevance of theology for the global crises of late-modernity. Our authors have been invited to introduce succinct and provocative arguments intended to provoke dialogue and exchange of ideas, while setting in relief the implications of theology for political and moral life.

Series Editors

Ashley John Moyse (PhD, Newcastle) is the McDonald Postdoctoral Fellow in Christian Ethics and Public Life, Christ Church, Oxford. In addition to his work with the Dispatches series, he has authored *Reading Karl Barth, Interrupting Moral Technique, Transforming Biomedical Ethics* (2015) and coedited several volumes, including *Correlating Sobornost: Conversations between Karl Barth and the Russian Orthodox Tradition* (Fortress, 2016), *Kenotic Ecclesiology: Select Writings of Donald M. MacKinnon* (Fortress, 2016), and *Treating the Body in Medicine and Religion: Jewish, Christian, and Islamic Perspectives* (forthcoming).

Scott A. Kirkland (PhD, Newcastle) is the inaugural postdoctoral research fellow and research coordinator for the Trinity College Theological School, University of Divinity, Melbourne. He is the author of *Into the Far Country: Karl Barth and the Modern Subject* (Fortress, 2016), coauthor, with John C. McDowell, of *Eschatology* (2018), and coeditor, with Ashley John Moyse and John C. McDowell, of *Correlating Sobornost: Conversations Between Karl Barth and the Russian Orthodox Tradition* (Fortress, 2016) and *Kenotic Ecclesiology: Select Writings of Donald M. MacKinnon* (Fortress, 2016).

Printed Titles

The End Is Not Yet by John W. de Gruchy
Political Orthodoxies by Cyril Hovorun

Forthcoming Titles

Gender Violence Church by Anna Mercedes
The Art of Living for a Technological Age by Ashley Moyse
Theology, Comedy, Politics by Marcus Pound
Intersectionality, Religion, and Theology by Joerg Rieger

Theology and the Globalized Present

Theology and the Globalized Present

Feasting in the Future of God

John C. McDowell

Fortress Press
Minneapolis

THEOLOGY AND THE GLOBALIZED PRESENT

Feasting in the Future of God

Cover image: © iStock / Nikada; Sagrada Familia Cathedral in Barcelona

Cover design: Alisha Lofgren

Paperback ISBN: 978-1-5064-3161-1

eBook ISBN: 978-1-5064-5611-9

The paper used in this publication meets the minimum requirements of American National Standard for Information Sciences — Permanence of Paper for Printed Library Materials, ANSI Z329.48-1984.

Manufactured in the U.S.A.

This book was produced using Pressbooks.com, and PDF rendering was done by PrinceXML.

To my children—
Archie, Jonathan, Joseph, Meg, and Robert.
May you remain hopeful in dark times

Contents

Acknowledgments

Several years ago I was given a new course to teach that had been designed with the title "Church and State." Working from Carl Schmitt's understanding of political theology, the course designer had undervalued the substantial shifts in the very nature of "the political," and was instead enamored by an archaic set of concerns about political sovereignty and the determinatively governing role of the state. Certainly matters of political sovereignty remain significant. Yet they do not do so in the sense of enabling questions about how "religion" is or is not legitimately able to participate in some neutral or stable "public arena," or by envisaging that it is through a consideration of statecraft that matters of justice, liberation, and responsibility are crucially best addressed. The image of the "arena" after all suggests a space already marked by, and for, conflict (either as gladiatorial or as sports arenas) or as a spectacular space for entertainment (concert arenas). The more interesting political questions today need to address what Henry Giroux, in a remarkable combination of images largely developed from Ulrich Beck, calls the "disimagination machine" of "zombie politics and casino capitalism." Suffice it to say that I renovated the course design in order to provide conditions for political reflections that are more attuned to the growing complexity and fluidity of the geopolitical response to a more fundamental form of discipline. This present book is animated by similar concerns about the nature of what Michel Foucault called disciplinary society that makes docile bodies, by the flows of neo-imperial power, by romanticized distractions of subjectivity that include attempts to speak in individuated terms of "authenticity," and by the conditions framing agential decision-making in contemporaneity.

In its earliest life this particular study emerged out of an invitation to present at a conference at Tyndale House in Cambridge in July 2001 on the theme of "Globalization." Two months prior to that I had tested the paper in the theological research seminar at St. Andrews University. That earlier occasion indicated a number of ways in which I needed to clarify my critical claims, particularly since an underlying nostalgic voice expressing a type of Luddism was mistakenly detected by one attendee, and an apologetic form of Christianity *contra mundum* by another. If there was a "luddite" moment it was less a technophobia and more a political questioning of the value *for persons' flourishing* of techno-progress and the disciplining of the cultural imagination. Another attendee criticized the lack of women cited in the study. While I take this as a timely warning about the danger of making claims concerning the global scope of Christian claims to well-being from distinctly limited perspectives, I would resist the cheap and intellectually shallow version of this type of criticism that reduces healing to matters of measurable quantity.

The material had subsequently lain dormant on my computer, during which time my research unpacked questions of hope more specifically in terms of Karl Barth's work, and I began to develop a political fascination with cultural and critical theory, especially in terms of the formation of hopeful subjects through popular forms of pedagogy offered by cinematic forms of representation. These years also witnessed significant changes in the global economy, with the economic slowdown and recessions of recent memory, the post-9/11 alienating of the stranger as suspected enemy, and the intensification of activities of torture and terror in a volatile geopolitical climate. In 2010 the joint ANZATS and MCD centenary conference invited me to offer a plenary keynote on the theme "God and the future." On the difficulties of comprehending and meaningfully using that phrase theologically I will have more to say later. For now, it is worth mentioning that this was the occasion not only for reconfiguring the paper, but also for catching the attention of Ashley Moyse who has since encouraged its expansion for the *Dispatches* series. My thanks to *Pacifica* for the initial publication ("Feastings in God at Midnight: Theology and the Globalised Present," *Pacifica* 23 [2011]: 299–321). I owe a debt of gratitude to Ashley and to Scott Kirkland not merely for the opportunity to return to this work, but also for the rich, provocative, energetic, insightful, and eminently stimulating intellectual conversations stretching back almost a decade.

This book forms a part of a larger project on the topic of hope, or at least hope in, to use Hannah Arendt's phrase, "dark times." But, it is not any kind of appeal to "hope." It is not hope if that means an evasion of difficulty and complexity, or of a rational foreclosing of the future. Hope is much needed—particularly a theological form of hopefulness born from the discipline of living faithfully in God's ways in Christ—but is seemingly in short supply. The alienating of the stranger as *alien* other and as *enemy* intensifies in an environment ever more fearful for its own security. Political economies reposition the state of exception, and the state of emergency has instead become the norm. Impatience with conversation, particularly deeply informed rational engagement, has been expressed in, among other things, the Trumping of democratic cooperation in radicalized politics of self-interest. The Brexiting of engagement from generous forms of moral responsibility for the well-being of near and distant neighbors in need continues in ever-increasing isolationist policies. Moreover, the question of what responsibility means in relation to need is most pertinent when "public" obligations are shrinking in consequence of a politics of scarcity/austerity for the many in contrast to the indulgence of the few. Finally, there is the disturbing matter of where agents of hope may emerge from when the churches, supposedly schools of Christian critique, are mired in scandal over activities of abuse, or have anemically succumbed to the flows of consumer culture. My study, as with all intellectual *responses*, comes too late. It comes too late to warn about the consequences of certain economic models and their generative wage disparities, atomized subjectivities activated by narcissistic self-protectionism, "democratic" voting in an oligarchic system of governance, heavy investments in the military-industrial machines and the engagement in permanent warfare, the erasure of genuinely critical conversation and interrogation in political affairs, and the reduction of God-talk to critically unaccountable habituations of belligerence or for justifying the way things go, or for politically evasive therapy for the individual soul. It comes too late to prevent the failure of reason and conversation to effectively challenge these named pressures on the global flourishing of mutually responsible life. Even though it may indeed come too late, it can only do what it hopes to do—and that is, to offer a modest witness to the advent of transfigured life. Hopefully it will not prove to be an academic luxury as a consequence. The book attempts to offer reasons for those in the framing of all things in, with, and under the saturation of the presence of the moment by the intensified forms of subjectivity construed in individuated terms, in the contemporary form of a disciplinary empire. Francis Fukuyama's reading of history is not at all adequately repaired by Samuel Huntington's thesis of a civilizational clash. Instead, an enmeshing of Aldous Huxley and George Orwell may prove to be more indicative of the nature of dominant disciplinary systems.

There are many who have contributed to keeping me hopeful. Several colleagues at the University of Divinity since 2015, especially Scott Kirkland, Suman Kashyap, and Fotini Toso. My family deserves a special mention; it provides significant support for my research, and endures my rantings when I slip into "lecture mode" on the theopolitical matters I engage with. I deeply appreciate the wisdom and patience of my wife Sandra. The book is dedicated to our children since it is they who are growing up in "dark times," and they whose developing ways in the world often require *leaps* of hope. But it would be remiss not to gratefully mention my parents John and Elizabeth, and my parents-in-law Rev. John and Margaret Carrick. It was from my late maternal grandfather Thomas Manson that I developed a distinct concern over binary exclusions, and over the injustices generated by irresponsible politics of blame against one's neighbors.

Finally, while my own playing season in 2017 has once again been blighted by significant injury, I have been truly invigorated by the energy, enthusiasm, maturity, intelligence, and passion of the lads I have had the privilege of coaching on the football (Association Football, that is!) field—Croydon Ranges Football Club Under 15 Reds. Invincible on the field in 2017, and thoroughly deserved Champions! May you long enrich the footballing culture of the state of Victoria.

John C. McDowell
University of Divinity
Melbourne, Australia

Preface: Now Is the Intellectual's Time

Politically Figuring the Intellectual

In the aftermath of the then recent carnage, Aldous Huxley's 1946 foreword to the reprint of *Brave New World* engages disdainfully with an academic reviewer of the book.[1] What have academics contributed to the flourishing of the world or to prevent the horrific onslaught? Perhaps, one might ask, what tune they were fiddling while the world burned down around them. This is a crucial matter that touches the heart of the academics' *raison d'être*, and is now no less pressing in the context of the remodeling of higher

1. Aldous Huxley, "Foreword," in *Brave New World* (London: Vintage, 2007), xli–l.

education when caught in the grip of corporate disciplining.[2] Huxley's intellectuals (and one must be careful not to slide the academic into the intellectual) are certainly deviants, unable to live within the system. Yet, in a very telling move, he domesticates any radical potential their labors might have by relegating their provocations to the hedonistic system so that they remain very much a part of the discipline provided by the dominant politico-cultural arrangements. Exile to Iceland appears to suit them fine.

It is easy for the hubristic ego of the academic to imagine that what she is doing is vital to the flourishing of life, in some form or another. The products of universities' self-marketing are frequently pervaded by grand claims for the significance of their research activities, and this is even with the aim of attempting to outdo their "rivals" as if they are football teams in a winner-takes-all competition, or are scrapping for the scarcest of resources in order to continue to survive and flourish. The business of enquiry in order to understand and cooperatively promote "knowledge"

2. See, e.g., Henry A. Giroux, *Dangerous Thinking in the Age of the New Authoritarianism* (London: Routledge, 2015), chs. 9–10; Henry A. Giroux and Susan Searls Giroux, *Take Back Higher Education: Race, Youth, and the Crisis of Democracy in the Post-Civil Rights Era* (New York: Palgrave Macmillan, 2004); Wendy Brown, *Undoing the Demos: Neoliberalism's Stealth Revolution* (New York: Zone Books, 2015), ch. 6; Zygmunt Bauman and Leonidas Donskis, *Moral Blindness: The Loss of Sensitivity in Liquid Modernity* (Cambridge: Polity, 2013), ch. 4; Bill Readings, *The University in Ruins* (Cambridge, MA: Harvard University Press, 1996); Gary Rolfe, *The University in Dissent* (Abingdon, UK: Routledge, 2013); Stanley Hauerwas, *The State of the University: Academic Knowledges and the Knowledge of God* (Oxford: Blackwell, 2007).

for the sake of human (rather than simply personal or institutional) flourishing is arguably not what much academic work is concerned with. Some years ago in a seminar in Cambridge's Divinity Faculty George Steiner termed the commentator a "parasite." This was a claim that had been given expression some years before in a paper titled "Humane Literacy." "The critic," he asserted in the latter, "lives at second-hand. He writes *about*. . . . [Consequently,] criticism exists by the grace of other men's genius."[3] In fact, in a poignant and politically significant turn, Steiner uses the image of the *too late*. Not only does the parasitical commentator fall well short of the genius of the artist, she cannot absent herself from a moral burden.

In pressing what that moral burden might involve, it is worth attending to another image that usefully depicts what occurs in the intellectual labors of critical reflection. The image emerges from comments made by Edward Said, and it is that of the intellectual being politically engaged in the borderlands of disciplinary discourses. With government pressure exerted on (the now "corporate") universities in the form of competition for funds from research data-collection exercises (especially in Australia where the *quantity* of each academic's output to be measured in the exercise is not capped) the scholar is largely reduced to the mechanized system of "battery research output," mass

3. George Steiner, *Language and Silence: Essays 1958-1967* (Harmondsworth, UK: Penguin, 1967), 21.

research production for research's sake.[4] Steiner's claim about "the retreat from the word" as involving "a brutalization and devaluation of the word in the mass-cultures and mass-politics of the age" is one that intensively resonates in the academic performance of contemporaneity.[5] Academia fiddles in the highly restrictive forms of professional specialization and technical formalism, in the "culture of critical discourse," through *pure peer-to-peer research* while Rome burns around it.[6] The "contemporary educated classes," it would appear, "have little or nothing to say about the desirable shape of the human condition."[7] So Said identifies a politically conservative turn in Western academia. "I think that's a transformation of the landscape as such now that the American left seems to have taken the easy alternative and has become largely academic and largely divorced from the world of intervention and the public realm, with a few exceptions."[8] Typically, "There is a danger that the figure or image of the intellectual might disappear in a mass

4. The striking image of "battery higher education" was used by Conrad Russell, cited in Richard H. Roberts, *Religion, Theology and the Human Sciences* (Cambridge: Cambridge University Press, 2002), 88.
5. Steiner, *Language and Silence*, 31, 67.
6. The phrase is that of Alvin W. Gouldner, *The Future of Intellectuals and the Rise of the New Class* (New York: Seabury, 1979), cited in Edward W. Said, *Representations of the Intellectual: The 1993 Reith Lectures* (New York: Vintage, 1994), 9.
7. Zygmunt Bauman, *Culture in a Liquid Modern World*, trans. Lydia Bauman (Cambridge: Polity, 2011), 49.
8. Edward W. Said, *The Pen and the Sword: Conversations with David Barsamian* (Edinburgh: AK Press, 1994), 168.

of details, and that the intellectual might become only another professional or a figure in a social trend."[9] In fact, Said laments, it is more likely that "today's intellectual . . . be a closeted literature professor, with a secure income, and no interest in dealing with the world outside the classroom."[10] The cardinal problem is a political one: that academic advancement becomes the focus of intellectual work rather than "social change." Of course, the corporatization of universities over the past two decades (i.e., after Said penned this criticism) has resulted in the replacement of many tenured academic positions with adjunct or part-time lecturing positions, and has rendered academic positions precarious by being tied more specifically to research "performance" and the achievement of external research income. Nonetheless, this precarious workforce is reduced to playing in increasingly conservative modes of institutional politics simply to be considered for ongoing work. The image of academia's own panopticon in Bauman's work depicts this in terms of "self-supervision and self-control by the objects of domination."[11]

Writing in the 1960s with the death knell of the *Shoah* still ringing in Europe's ears, Steiner reminds his readers of the fact that all criticism comes "after, and

9. Said, *Representations of the Intellectual*, 11. "In the end as a full specialized literary intellectual you become tame and accepting of whatever the so-called leaders in the field will allow" (77).
10. Said, *Representations of the Intellectual*, 70.
11. Bauman, *Culture in a Liquid Modern World*, 55.

that is the nerve of our condition" in the aftermath of "the unprecedented ruin of humane values and hopes by the political bestiality of our age."[12] What this means, he continues, is that "we cannot act now, be it as critics or merely as rational beings, as if nothing of vital relevance had happened to our sense of the human possibility, as if the extermination by hunger or violence of some seventy million men, women and children in Europe and Russia between 1914 and 1945 had not altered, profoundly, the quality of our awareness." Some within the academy continue to long for the positive political significance of their labors, and that is precisely what Said attempts to undertake in his own work in the borderlands when exposing the politically determinative ideological operations of, among other things, "orientalism." Such an endeavor, of course, demands that critical purchase be made on academic attempts to police the borders between disciplines. So Said claims, "Yet there will always remain the perennial escape mechanism of saying that a literary scholar and a philosopher, for example, are trained in literature and philosophy respectively, not in politics or ideological analysis. In other words, the specialist argument can work quite effectively to block the larger and, in my opinion, the more intellectually serious perspective."[13]

12. Steiner, *Language and Silence*, 22.
13. Edward W. Said, *Orientalism: Western Conceptions of the Orient* (London: Penguin, 1978), 13.

This passage weaves a rich tapestry of suggestion and possibility, all the more important for the fact that this writer challenges the exclusion of certain potentially disruptive voices in the conversation. "Orientalism," he maintains, is a discourse freighted with unacknowledged assumptions. These assumptions are culturally specific (belonging to the descriptions made by the western European imperial powers of the nineteenth century and early twentieth century); imperialist (imposing a descriptive vision upon others, albeit in the main it is countenanced by the latter rather than violently imposed upon them, a program of ideological pacification that largely accounts for its durability); derived from and subsequently enhancing a positional privileging (the European imperial powers "civilize" what they regard as "primitive" or underdeveloped regions); naturalized and therefore existing in a state of denial with regard to the constructed nature of these assumptions that reinforce compartmentalization and consequently resist possibilities of genuine cultural and social exchange; and practically determinative (creative of certain possibilities for the shape of policymaking). This is a fruitful ideology in the sense that not only does it yield new sets of possibilities for acting, but it also reinforces itself by producing an exclusive and secure way for thinking. So, Said declares, "Orientalism's power and effectiveness . . . everywhere remind the reader that henceforth in order to get at the Orient he must pass through the learned grids and codes provided by the Orientalist."[14] Furthermore, defining the good and its flourishing for the subjugated culture lies not in its own hands. The subjugated lose their self-descriptive voice and their ability to resist and correct the identifying system of judgment imposed upon them.

The colonial scheme is hereby founded on, and sustained by, a pronounced anthropological duality of an "us" and a "them," of a "self" and an "other." This paternalistic perspective on colonial presence and action is displayed, for example, in Arthur James Balfour's House of Commons speech of June 13, 1910, in which he announces that the Egyptian "them" "have got it far better" under the British imperial government "than in the whole history of the world they ever had before, and which not only is a benefit to them, but is undoubtedly a benefit to the whole of the civilized West. We," he continues, "are in Egypt not merely for the sake of the Egyptians, though we are there for their sake; we are there also for the sake of Europe at large."[15] "Our" rule, this expression of colonial ideology assumes, is for "their" betterment. Balfour speaks glowingly, then, "of all the loss of which we have relieved the population and . . . all the benefits which we have given to them," and of Britain as exporting "our very best to these countries." While far from seeking to create possibilities of exoneration

14. Said, *Orientalism*, 67.
15. Said, *Orientalism*, 33.

for those involved "with this rather sordid experience of imperialism," what this nevertheless amounts to is for Said an indication of modern European imperialism that cannot simply be demonized through a "politics of blame," a response that equally trades on an (colonial) "other."[16] There is both the complicity of the subjugated in the imperialistic ideology, the occasional good intentions of the imperialists, and the imperial succumbing to a whole set of ideological assumptions. There is a very real sense, then, in which this form of imperialism not only insidiously affects and "creates" those who are subjugated by it, but also manufactures the very people who serve it. In other words, while this ideology in some senses has a certain broad coherence with features of the world it purports to describe, it says significantly more about the worldviews of its advocates. The world of the "Orient" itself is largely rendered mute and thereby unable to resist or surprise the projects, images, or mere descriptions devised for it.

Developing such a critical perspective on all this is a feat made possible by paying serious attention to particularity—to the particularity of those described and, as it transpires, misdescribed by this discourse of Orientalism and those who do the describing and misdescribing. In particular, Said attempts to open up time for listening to a multiplicity of previously silenced

16. Edward W. Said, *Culture and Imperialism* (New York: Vintage, 1993), 70.

voices, voices drowned out by the controlling master-narrative. This movement of giving sight to those "blind to other histories" in itself, then, becomes a form of resistance.[17] Resisting the discursive hegemony becomes, it should be added, a morally significant matter that is shaped by the construction of alternative visions or ways of telling the story that more comprehensively incorporate and *retain* the distinctiveness of these voices.[18] Incorporating these voices into the dominating master-narrative is an analysis characterized by a certain exteriority to what it describes. This means that the subverting morality of *witness* involves a responsibility to open up the conversation in a way that resists the hegemony of monologue. And it does this not for its own sake, as if suspicion is to give way to cynicism, but for the sake of better integration.

Moreover, as the first lengthy citation above declares, subverting this hegemony imposed and adopted is a task broader than what is made possible in the agencies of politically trained ideology-analysts. It is of a piece with the responsibility to tell well the stories of our lives and those of others who claim to representationally speak in our place, that the contemporary proliferation of specialisms cannot release the

17. Citation from Said, *Culture and Imperialism*, xix.

18. Good reflections on the moral integrity of *conversing* with others in refusal to foreclose discourse against potentially disruptive voices can be found in Rowan Williams, *On Christian Theology* (Oxford: Blackwell, 2000), ch. 1.

so-called amateur from responsibility to probe, interrogate, and imagine matters differently. This claim can be broken down into the following two broad claims: in the first place, the matter is much too *ethically important* to be left to specialists, and thus cannot properly be dealt with at the rather thin and distorting hermetic level of the "history of ideas"; and in the second place, even those identified as specialists are not free from the formative operation of special "interests." It is worth quoting Said again at some length on this:

> The determining impingement on most knowledge produced in the contemporary United States . . . is that it be nonpolitical, that is, scholarly, academic, impartial, above partisan or small-minded doctrinal belief. One can have no quarrel with such an ambition in theory, perhaps, but in practice the reality is much more problematic. No one has ever devised a method for detaching the scholar from the circumstances of life, from the fact of his involvement (conscious or unconscious) with a class, a set of beliefs, a social position, or from the mere activity of being a member of a society. These continue to bear on what he does professionally, even though naturally enough his research and his fruits do attempt to reach a level of relative freedom from the inhibitions and the restrictions of brute, everyday reality. For there is no such thing as knowledge that is less, rather than more, partial than the individual (with his entangling and distracting life circumstances) who produces it. Yet this knowledge is not therefore automatically nonpolitical. . . . What I am interested in doing now is suggesting

> how the general liberal consensus that "true" knowledge is fundamentally nonpolitical (and conversely, that overtly political knowledge is not "true" knowledge) obscures the highly if obscurely organized political circumstances obtaining when knowledge is produced.[19]

The Politics of Cultural Work in Dark Times

Where Said speaks of "the public role of the intellectual as outsider, 'amateur,' and disturber of the status quo," an equally potentially useful image in this connection is that of "teachers as cultural workers." It is a claim made by critical educationalist Paolo Freire in his work on identifying and transforming pedagogies that undemocratically oppress and dehumanize as a result of the vested power "interests of the oppressors."[20] If Freire has been able to successfully make and sustain a case for the role of teachers in the process of transformative learning, a quite significant way of construing cultural analysis and criticism becomes necessary, as Grace Jantzen argues. She characterizes "the west as [being caught] in the grip of a cultural neurosis of which its death-dealing structures are symptoms," and this entails "[that] the task of the intellectual can be

19. Said, *Orientalism*, 10.
20. Said, *Representations of the Intellectual*, x. See Paolo Freire, *Teachers as Cultural Workers: Letters to Those Who Dare Teach*, trans. Donaldo Macedo, Dale Koike, and Alexandre Oliveira (Boulder, CO: Westview, 2005); *Pedagogy of the Oppressed* (New York: Continuum, 1990), 39.

likened to that of a therapist who seeks by patient listening to bring the repressed dimensions of history to the fore and to release the springs of wellbeing."[21] The generalizing and cliché-ridden rhetoric of "the West" here certainly requires substantial analysis since it is too neat, prone to herding too much into its stock conceptualization, and thereby precariously vulnerable to disruption by discordant voices. The more useful point, however, is that Jantzen's sense of requisite political therapy involves considerably more than the provision of arguments. So she recognizes that if one can treat the troubles of the contemporary West "as an obsession or psychic disorder of the social realm, then it will not be changed by arguing against it."[22] The problems, depicted as neuroses, are far too deeply learned and conditioned for that to be the case. "Appeals to rationality will not bring about the desired change, any more than it would help to tell a person in the grip of a neurosis what it is that they are repressing. Such strategies only bring out stronger resistance, ever more clever rationalizations, deeper anger and control."[23] In contrast, she maintains, bringing "about human flourishing . . . requires substantial change in material as well as discursive conditions, changes in behaviour as well as in thought."[24] However, lest the

21. Grace M. Jantzen, *Foundations of Violence: Death and the Displacement of Beauty* (London: Routledge, 2004), 4.
22. Jantzen, *Foundations of Violence*, 19.
23. A similar point is made by Kenneth Surin, *Freedom Not Yet: Liberation and the Next World Order* (Durham, NC: Duke University Press, 2009), 6.

cultural commentator despair at the magnitude of the task of criticism and properly transformative repair, Jantzen indicates the need for "patient investigation and analysis" over the shape and content of the beliefs that form or enculturate our sensibilities and that thereafter regulate our imaginations and practical judgments.[25]

> What we can learn from the therapeutic model is that to the extent that the problems of post/modernity are consequences of acting upon a destructive cultural symbolic, strategies and policies to change behaviour are unlikely to be effective unless the underlying patterns of thought are changed. Moreover for this to happen it is necessary to bring those patterns, the cultural symbolic, to consciousness, and this, in therapy, means probing its sources and history. Once the contours of the symbolic become clearer it becomes easier to see what is involved in its transformation and why it is necessary to go through the massive process of tracing its past in order to redeem the present.[26]

The cultural symbolic of Western societies and the options for social order that are made possible as a consequence require observation, analysis, and critique. The aim is not to simply "understand," as if knowledge is separate from hope and planning, or in order to achieve some nebulous "cultural/media liter-

24. Jantzen, *Foundations of Violence*, 19.
25. Jantzen, *Foundations of Violence*, 19.
26. Jantzen, *Foundations of Violence*, 19.

acy." After all, as Stanley Aronowitz argues, "without agency there can be no history except an automatic kind."[27] The key to practices of transformative pedagogy is to resist the loss of agency, and therefore the reduction of hope to something not focused on the flourishing of all things together. In that way, academic reflection and critical thought can serve creaturely flourishing as a "critical condition" and not become a self-referential substitute for sociopolitical engagement for constructive change.[28] It is to emerge as a contribution to orientating "us in the darkness."[29] In fact, Jantzen would grandly reconfigure this in soteriological terms given the critic's role in identifying that "the world is in sore need of redemption."[30] Of course, even to make such a claim is to already position oneself, to have a perspective, and it is important not to be naïve about the legitimacy of such soteriological claims lest they too become discursive impositions of one's perspective. This means that the critical condition attempts as best as it can not to slip into typically naïve appeals to political neutrality but maintain a self-aware "state of constant alertness."[31] After all, according to Said, "modern empire requires, as Conrad

27. Stanley Aronowitz, *The Politics of Identity: Class, Culture, Social Movements* (New York: Routledge, 1992), 11.
28. The phrase is taken from Wendy Brown, *Edgework: Critical Essays on Knowledge and Politics* (Princeton: Princeton University Press, 2005), 7.
29. Brown, *Edgework*, 15.
30. Jantzen, *Foundations of Violence*, 3.
31. Citation from Said, *Representations of the Intellectual*, 23.

said, an idea of service, an idea of sacrifice, an idea of redemption. Out of this you get these great, massively reinforced notions of, for example, in the case of France, the '*Mission civilisatrice*.' That we're not there to benefit ourselves, we're there for the sake of the natives."[32] While it will be left for now largely as an assertion rather than as an argument, it is worth citing Stanley Hauerwas's observation that, whether it is acknowledged or not, "all education . . . is moral formation."[33] Indeed, "Education and pedagogy do not exist outside of relations of power, values, and politics."[34] Pedagogies, whether through educative practices of writing, classroom instruction, or some other media, are never politically innocent.[35] Rather, they enact judgments regarding what is valuable, and perform ways of encoding, using, and generating forms of power. What this entails, Said maintains, is that "the intellectual who claims to write only for him or herself, or for the sake of pure learning, or abstract science is not to be, and *must not* be, believed."[36] A pedagogy of

32. Said, *The Pen and the Sword*, 66.
33. Stanley Hauerwas, *The State of the University: Academic Knowledges and the Knowledge of God* (Malden, MA: Blackwell, 2007), 46.
34. Henry Giroux, *America at War with Itself* (San Francisco: City Lights, 2017), 250. Cf. Freire, *Pedagogy of the Oppressed*, 56.
35. On the formative effects of cultural representations, or schooling without the boundaries of the school, for instance, see Ivan Illich, *Deschooling Society* (London: Marion Boyars, 1970), 29, 39; Henry A. Giroux, *Breaking into the Movies: Film and the Culture of Politics* (Malden, MA: Blackwell, 2002); *The Violence of Organized Forgetting: Thinking Beyond America's Disimagination Machine* (San Francisco: City Lights, 2014), 50.
36. Said, *Representations of the Intellectual*, 110.

political attentiveness occurs only as "educators . . . not only critically question and register their own subjective involvement in how and what they teach, but also resist all calls to depoliticize learning."[37] It is for this reason that Freire reflects on liberative pedagogical practices for the oppressed, and contests forms of education that induct learners into the logic of the present system where that system operates through forms of hegemonic practices and values.

37. Giroux, *America at War with Itself*, 250.

Introduction: The Future of God

To offer both a preface and an introduction might appear to overburden the prelude to the main event. The former has largely functioned as a throat-clearing exercise, or the tuning of the instruments prior to the overture. It has attempted to lay at the door of academia both the need for, and the unavoidability of, political attention. By considering the nature of intellectual responsibility to orient us in dark times, to appeal again to Wendy Brown's image adapted from Hannah Arendt, the earlier material has attempted to frame the book around the sense of political urgency the *Dispatches* series inhabits. Without the ability to think dangerously in public, one would not "have to live in an overtly totalitarian country to be corrupted by the formative culture that makes it possible."[1]

O Brave New World That Has Such (Self-Subjected) People in It

As we move closer to articulating the theme of the book, it is worth commencing with a gesture toward what the study is doing by returning to Huxley's foreword. For him *Brave New World* is about "the future."[2] By this he does not mean to suggest that his narrative has provided a futurological forecast couched in a predictive voice. After all, the opening of the foreword announces the political significance of art, and Huxley's reflections on what he would rewrite in his original narrative, if he were to do so, largely focus on political and religious matters. The author's interest is, therefore, less in the details regarding the yet-to-come technologies as to the values, desires, ends, of those who use them, and of the absorption of persons into those technologies that not merely express value but regulate and manufacture values in such a way as to contribute to the making of sociopolitically conformist persons. One of his observations of what kind of repair might be offered involves couching "the Savage," the representative figure of the sane community living in exile on the borderlands of the brave new world, as exhibiting a markedly different relationship to technologies than those habituated within the brave new

1. Henry A. Giroux, *Dangerous Thinking in the Age of the New Authoritarianism* (London: Routledge, 2015), 15.
2. Aldous Huxley, *Brave New World* (London: Vintage, 2007), xliii.

world's political order. In this regard, the reconfigured relationship would entail that technologies "had been made for man, not (as at present and still more so in brave new world) as though man were to be adapted and enslaved to them."[3] Huxley here is more attuned to ways in which the relations cannot be considered *expressly* in terms of simple *use*. His narrative offers something of an extended meditation on the manner in which technologies *condition* perceptions, *form* character and social processes, and thereby *transform* and *regulate* knowledge and value. As Neil Postman argues, "Every technology has a philosophy, which is given expression in how the technology makes people use their minds, in what it makes us do with our bodies, in how it codifies the world, in which of our senses it amplifies, in which of our emotional and intellectual tendencies it disregards."[4] The depiction of the Reservation *community* as "a society composed of freely cooperating individuals devoted to the pursuit of sanity" somewhat mitigates the more romanticized elements of Huxley's narrative depiction. It operates as a contrast to a less sane form of collectivity operating in, with, and under the efficient direction of "highly centralized totalitarian governments," of an enslaving, conditioning, but noncoercive system of control that loves servitude, or control by socially stabilizing

3. Huxley, *Brave New World*, xliii.
4. Neil Postman, *The End of Education: Redefining the Value of School* (New York: Vintage, 1995), 192.

governance that provides the conditions for a hedonistic culture.[5] Huxley's is a vision of the destruction of what he liberally calls "a race of free individuals," and his art is a warning about, and a call for attentiveness to, the conditions that generate it.[6]

In his rich study of globalization Jean-Luc Nancy is concerned with a unitive system of globality that processes life in such a way that it generates the destruction of that very life. This *globalization* he contrasts with *mondialization* or "world-forming."[7] In fact, the former is depicted as the "suppression of all world-forming of the world," the world's very self-destruction in the forming of the unworld.[8] Globalization he defines as "an enclosure in the undifferentiated sphere of a unitotality," and, he continues, that biopolitics which "has already translated everything in a global idiom."[9] This he adjudges to be the dominating assertion of "an empire made up of technological power and pure economic reason," the sweeping circulation of everything by the market "in the form of commodity."[10] Such a totalizing translation constitutes in no uncertain terms a nihilistic logic, "an unprecedented geopolitical, economic, and ecological catastro-

5. Huxley, *Brave New World*, xliii, xlvii.
6. Huxley, *Brave New World*, l.
7. Jean-Luc Nancy, *The Creation of the World or Globalization*, trans. François Raffoul and David Pettigrew (Albany: State University of New York Press, 2007), 29.
8. Nancy, *The Creation of the World*, 50, 34. See 35.
9. Nancy, *The Creation of the World*, 28.
10. Nancy, *The Creation of the World*, 34, 37.

phe" that makes "the unworld."[11] Out of its multiple deformations and death-drive it is worth highlighting Nancy's sense that from its generation of wealth comes "a worsening of inequalities of all sorts within these populations—economic, biological and cultural."[12]

What, among other things, is intriguing, is the fact that the world becomes "immanent . . . to itself" in Nancy's positive repair, that takes the form of announcing the undecidability of the world's excessive self-constructive becoming a subject, who is being-in-the-world, in *mondialization*.[13] This is creation and re-creation, the work of justice that is always the to-come of an *ex nihilo* creativity. "God annihilates itself as a 'self' or as a distinct being in order to 'withdraw' in its act—which makes the opening of the world."[14] As with Huxley's novel, there is no future for God, or at least no "god" if by that is meant an ontotheologically depictable form of transcendence who enables representation of the world.

The Future of God or God's Future?

As with all theological claims, whether they take the form of a potential sound bite or not, language of "the future of God" requires substantial complicating work

11. Nancy, *The Creation of the World*, 50, 34.
12. Nancy, *The Creation of the World*, 34.
13. Nancy, *The Creation of the World*, 41.
14. Nancy, *The Creation of the World*, 70.

to be done. Part of the task, then, is not to simplify. What is not meant by that, however, is that the verbosity of academic performance should blight the theological presentation with undue rhetorical complication. As Nicholas Lash once argued, there is no virtue in ugly theological writing.[15] Rather, the type of simplification that needs to be contested has more to do with the refusal to permit the Real to be perceived in all its complexity and excessiveness. This is the simplism expressed in the work of glib theologies. With Dan Hardy, what is required is an awareness that "it is a complexity which reaches far into the heart of the issues," the kind of complexity that is missed by those who are "too fond of simplicities and the comfort they bring."[16]

Hardy began his symposium paper with an acknowledgment of the presumptuousness of the title he had been given, "The Future of Theology in a Complex World," and announced his unfitness to address it. Something similar could be claimed for my book's subtitle, which involves the phrase "the future of God."

Talk of "the future of God" could do at least two kinds of intellectual work. To explain this it is instructive to take a detour into the phrase "God is dead." In *The Gay Science* Friedrich Nietzsche's madman Moses-

15. Nicholas Lash in a private conversation (1995).
16. Daniel W. Hardy, "The Future of Theology in a Complex World: An Opening to Discussion," in *God's Ways with the World: Thinking and Practising Christian Faith* (Edinburgh: T&T Clark, 2005), 22.

like ascends a mountain and famously, or infamously, announces that "God is dead" and we have killed him. On his descent from the mountain-experience he discovers the particular idolatry of the village crowd. Their affirmation of the theological negation nonetheless curtails its proper impact—they live as closet theists, continuing on as if God lives, as if nothing has happened. At this point the madman's speech looks anguished with his brief panic-stricken questions, and his apocalyptic allusions to the whole "sequence of breakdown, ruin, and cataclysm that is now impending" for "the whole of our European morality."[17] This parabolic moment suggests an ambiguity in the meaning of the claim "God is dead."

In the first place, the statement seems to make a sociocultural observation, an assertion about what has been named "secularization." "God" is irrelevant to sociocultural conditions. Accordingly, to switch back to our theme, God has no future for Nietzsche and for late nineteenth-century European society. As Charles Taylor recognizes, "the countries of western Europe have mainly become secular—even those who retain the vestigial public reference to God in public space."[18] In this regard, however, recent reflections on the "reenchantment" of the world significantly suggest that all is not well with mapping onto the present any

17. Friedrich Nietzsche, *The Gay Science*, trans. Walter Kaufmann (New York: Vintage, 1974), 343; cf. 125.
18. Charles Taylor, *A Secular Age* (Cambridge, MA: Belknap, 2007), 2.

kind of secularization thesis without substantive remodeling. This "return" of the religious to even the most public places can be documented through various phenomenological studies, and accounts can be provided of the disenchantment with the so-called "secular project" itself in its own totalizing, demythologizing discourse. In fact, Graham Ward and Michael Hoelzl claim not merely that the secularization thesis no longer applies to contemporary conditions, but that it has always been flawed. So they argue that "what we are experiencing [is not] a re-emergence of religion, but a new visibility—a visibility that is far more complex and nuanced than the simple re-emergence of something that has been in decline in the past but is now manifesting itself once more."[19] That thesis suggests that "religion" has not disappeared as a version of the secularization thesis imagined it would. Lash observes that "notwithstanding the best efforts of d'Hollbach or Feuerbach, however, people have not ceased to 'believe in God.'" "But," Lash continues, "belief has never been so dangerously ambivalent. Each US dollar bill still bears the message 'In God we trust.'"[20] "Secularization" looks less sufficient as an explanatory paradigm, and it needs to be substantially modified in light of the fact that in most places, espe-

19. Graham Ward and Michael Hoelzl, introduction to *The New Visibility of Religion: Studies in Religion and Cultural Hermeneutics*, ed. Graham Ward and Michael Hoelzl (London: Continuum, 2008), 1–11 (1).
20. Nicholas Lash, *Theology for Pilgrims* (London: Darton, Longman & Todd, 2008), 40.

cially in the non-West, religious traditions and practices remain strong, and if anything are growing. So, for instance, argues Peter Berger, "The rapid spread of Charismatic Christianity around the globe [and particularly in Latin America] in the twentieth century and beyond has confounded secularization theory which had predicted the demise of religion at the level both of individual practice and of social and political influence."[21] Moreover, Berger continues, "resurgent Islam is the most vital, vibrant and growing form of religion in the world today."[22] But not only is this true of the non-West. While Europe continues to be something of the exceptional case, according to Grace Davie, since it still powerfully exhibits the presence of secularization, there are also signs of something quite different emerging—what commentators are calling "the re-enchantment of the [Western] world."[23] Consequently, Malory Nye observes that

> The contemporary world is shaped by religions: the "war on terror," intelligent design, abortion clinic killings, Waco, conflicts and wars in the Middle East, India, former Yugoslavia, Northern Ireland, the Jonestown mass suicides, environmental summits, peace

21. Peter L. Berger, "Secularization and De-Secularization," in *Religions in the Modern World*, ed. Linda Woodhead et al. (London: Routledge, 2002), 291–98 (293).
22. Berger, "Secularization and De-Secularization," 293.
23. Graham Ward, *True Religion* (Oxford: Blackwell, 2003), 130. Cf. Grace Davie, *Europe: The Exceptional Case. Parameters of Faith and the Modern World* (London: Darton, Longman & Todd, 2000).

> demonstrations—the list goes on. Hardly a day goes by when there is not some manifestation of religion (religious identity, religious practice, religious conflict) reported on the TV or in newspapers. To understand the contemporary world, as well as the past, we need a sophisticated understanding of religion.[24]

On the one hand, for example, identifiably religious themes saturate the popular media, and not merely in the more explicitly religious, such as with Mel Gibson's *Passion of the Christ* and *The Da Vinci Code*, but in shows like *The Simpsons*, the Harry Potter series, the Star Wars saga, the rebooted *Battlestar Galactica*, *The Walking Dead*, the reimagining of vampire mythology, the appeal of the magical and even the superhero popularity, and so on. On the other, the West is also witnessing the rise of what George Steiner calls "the nostalgia for the absolute" in the form of assertive forms of religious fundamentalisms, Christian, Hindu, and Islamic.[25] According to Harvey Cox, "Paradoxically, by some standards the world may be even less secular at the end of the twentieth century than it was at the beginning. . . . In many places [even] in Europe today one gets the distinct impression that although the *institutional* forms of religions may be weaker than they once were, religion still plays a strong role in public culture."[26]

24. Malory Nye, *Religion: The Basics*, 2nd ed. (London: Routledge, 2004), 1.
25. Citation from the title of George Steiner, *The Nostalgia for the Absolute* (Toronto: Anansi, 1974).

Yet what this means, or rather precisely what "returns" or, to refer to Ward and Hoelzl's descriptor, becomes "visible," has to be attended to with considerably more care than rather glib appeals to the situation being hopeful allow for. The conditions for reflection on religions are complex, and no simple definitions of what "religion" is will currently suffice, as if the multiplicities can be reduced to a simple nonparticularizing account of indifference to differences. Certainly we would do well to complicate David Tracy's claim that "postmodern theology is an honest if sometimes desperate attempt to let God as God be heard again."[27] Just how far *Theos* has returned as interrupting and destabilizing the dominant modern *logos* is far from clear. Postmodernities—and some versions of these are bound up with the logic of late capitalist consumer subjectivity—are too diffuse and unstable to be accorded the status, without pause, of theological ally without falling into glib discourse such as Tracy does when he asserts further that "postmodernity provided a new opportunity for serious contemporary thought on God."[28] What emerges is, among other things,

26. Harvey Cox, "The Myth of the Twentieth Century: The Rise and Fall of 'Secularization,'" in *The Twentieth Century: A Theological Overview*, ed. Gregory Baum (Maryknoll, NY: Orbis, 1999), 135–43 (136, 138).
27. David Tracy, "The Return of God in Contemporary Theology," in Claude Geffré and Werner Jeanrond, *Why Theology?* Concilium Series (London: SCM, 1994), 37–46 (38).
28. Tracy, "The Return of God in Contemporary Theology," 42.

a multiplicity of diffuse late-capitalist spiritualities for consumer satisfaction.

Cox argues that "atheism and rationalism no longer constitute (if they ever really did) the major challenge to . . . theology today. The challenge comes not from the death of God but from the 're-birth of the gods' (and the goddesses!)."[29] The most important challenge for Cox is, then, the pluralistic religious environment. However, the challenges for the so-called traditional religious faiths in the contemporary postsecular condition is perhaps more significant than merely having to contend with multiple religions. After all, Islam, Judaism, and Christianity were all born into the religious syncretisms of the Arabian Peninsula, the Fertile Crescent, and the Hellenized Roman Empire respectively.

Much of the "liquid" spirituality or religiosity in the West today largely takes place outside of religious institutions and is pathologically consumerist in spirit while designated as a genuine option for a tolerant age—it involves an eclectic blend of religious stories and practices, diffusely constructed around the individual's needs or desires for satisfaction, or for the palliative effect of soothing a beleaguered soul, or the expression of boredom with fractured forms of living.

> There is what Robert Wuthnow has called "patchwork religion." In one study after another in . . . [the West]

29. Cox, "The Myth of the Twentieth Century," 140.

> one finds people who put together an individualized religion, taking bits and pieces from different traditions, and coming up with a religious profile that does not fit easily into any of the organized denominations. Many of them assert that they are not "religious" at all, but are pursuing a quest for "spirituality." Very similar data come up in European research. Hervieu-Léger uses Claude Lévi-Strauss's term *bricolage* to describe this form of religiosity—people putting together a religion of their own like children tinkering with a lego set, picking and choosing from the available religious "material."[30]

So in demythologizing mode Ward argues that "what we are witnessing is not a return [of religion] but a new religiousness that is hybrid, fluid, and commercialized."[31] This customized and bourgeois form of religiosity is, he continues, a "liquid" spirituality narcissistically customized for a lifestyle role for those accustomed to the culturally bombarding propaganda of "choosing" their leisure and entertainment. Similarly Cox claims that this is not the "resacralization" of the Western world, or the return of the religions, so much as "a fascinating *transformation of religion*, a creative series of self-adaptations by religions to the new conditions created by the modernity some of them helped to spawn." [32] In other words, the contemporary situation may well challenge the dominance

30. Berger, "Secularization and De-Secularization," 295.
31. Graham Ward, *The Politics of Discipleship: Becoming Postmaterial Citizens* (Grand Rapids: Baker Academic, 2009), 131.
32. Cox, "The Myth of the Twentieth Century," 139.

of the secular paradigm, but it presents a number of significant difficulties for those seeking to live within and to promote the so-called "traditional" religious faiths, those for whom their tradition is a "way of life" rather than the politically innocuous chosen religious lifestyle.

Nonetheless, intellectual reflection on these matters becomes, in this first way of understanding "the future of God," subject to a phenomenological reduction.[33] Talking of the "future of God," the term "God" of course then functioning metonymously, is bound up with processes of futurism, of projective reflections on contemporary trends and planning. Such an endeavor is, to the degree that trends are the best we have for fragilely reflecting on the shape of the future, speculative and theologically uninteresting, except perhaps when questions and assumptions concerning human identity are concerned.

Yet, in the second place, the madman's negation can be read philosophically as making an ontological claim. Death has to do with nonexistence, nonliveliness, or generativeness as much as with social regulativeness. It refers to a predicate that God has—not so much a divine perfection as the perfecting of philosophy and thus of God-talk. "God is dead" here suggests that the

33. At its most reductionist, phenomenological approaches since the nineteenth century have envisaged Theology as an impossible (because it has no "object") and a dishonest (because it continues without admitting that) intellectual discipline.

theological has been exposed as having no subject-matter. In this vein, talk of "the future of God" would be making an ontological claim, with "future" becoming, in some shape or form, a predicate of "God." The language itself would philosophically contest the Nietzschean since for God to have a future, whatever that might mean theologically, God is not mortified, not "dead." Nonetheless, the contestation cannot be a straightforward one. The first approach suggested in the ambiguity of the phrase "the future of God" can complicate matters by adverting to the plurality of theological discourses. From this it becomes clear that one cannot assume that we all mean the same thing by "God," a mistake often made by certain forms of comparative religion and secular humanism (in its opposition to so-called "religion") and modern theism, among others. So Michael J. Buckley argues that "'God' has become so sentimentally amorphous that it admits any statement of meaning, even quite contradictory statements, and can be applied to any treasured phenomenon or friend behind the phenomenon."[34]

When one does use the term in relation to the One whom Christians worship, the God of Jesus Christ, what does it mean to predicate futurity of God? There are several accounts within this family of post-Hegelian theological ontologies. These range from Teilhard de Chardin's largely progressivist teleology of

34. Michael J. Buckley, *At the Origins of Modern Atheism* (New Haven: Yale University Press, 1987), 13.

Christ as the world's Omega Point, through the world-experientializing of God in Process Theologies such as that of Norman Pittinger, to the reciprocative God–world agencies that enable the Self-limiting suffering of God as in Jürgen Moltmann, and the ontology of the coming of God from the future as in Wolfhart Pannenberg.

Theology and the Globalized Present will not directly address either of these broad and methodologically distinct approaches as such, but will dogmatically relocate talk of "the future *of* God" in talk of the world's future *in* God, in God's creativeness expressed in hopeful performance. The context for the theological discussion is the significant pressure on possibilities not merely for the shape of hope but also of the very existence of hope, generated by the detemporalized conditions for the making of selves in a "globalized" environment. Modernity's latest expression is closing the capacity for speaking adequately of the time required to become human, "real time." As Rowan Williams suggests, selfhood and temporality are deeply connected: "the erosions of selfhood in North Atlantic modernity, and . . . the accompanying erosion of certain ways of imagining *time*."[35] This requires substantive ethical attention, conversation, and interrogation simply because it arguably renders fundamental possibilities for the shaping of human selfhood increasingly

35. Rowan Williams, *Lost Icons: Reflections on Cultural Bereavement* (Edinburgh: T&T Clark, 2000), 8.

unavailable. As Zygmunt Bauman argues, globalization is an "ethical challenge."[36] In response a theological vision is reimagined to offer a constructive retemporalizing interrogation and eschatological memory, and the suggestions for beginning that are teased out broadly with reference to e ucharistic performance. Contrary to many expectations, this entails *not so much a dreaming of a different world* as a *dreaming of this world differently*. The theological materials are not offered as a flight from thought, or a flight into feeling, or a securing of feeling through theological consolation.[37] Rather, they offer a temporality that is hope-generating, is critically attentive to the inequitable character of features of our world, and is educative of ethical wisdom in a self-regulating and emancipatory witness of remembering and anticipating the transformative presence of God.

The Chapters

The heavy critical analysis is undertaken in chapter 1 in order to maintain that the contemporary global economy overspills any attempt to seclude and contain

36. Zygmunt Bauman, *Does Ethics Have a Chance in a World of Consumers?* (Cambridge, MA: Harvard University Press, 2008), 71.
37. Kathryn Tanner laments, "Christians [themselves] have employed beliefs about God and the world to hamper developments of the attitudes necessary for outrage against injustice and sustained efforts to remedy it." *The Politics of God: Christian Theologies and Social Justice* (Minneapolis: Fortress Press, 1992), 2.

it within a purely economic sphere. The material tackles the nature of the disciplining of desire, imagination, and agency, the temporality and the nature of what is and is not free about the "free" global market economy. The economy reconfigures the very nature of *time*, the time to become and be human, the time for global flourishing. The second chapter turns to the production of waste, of that which is *necessarily* rendered disposable within and because of the market economy. Chapter 3 considers one possible form of resistance that turns out, in the end, to be rather toothless as a resistant site for the generation of hope, "religion." This form of resistance is problematic precisely because it operates from within a commodified option. The interest of the fourth chapter lies in the capacity of the eucharist to function as a resistant time-making practice, a prominent theological response to the discipline of the global market in much recent theological literature. If this claim is to have any purchase, however, it must engage in rigorous theological interrogation that delineates the eucharist's eschatologically dangerous memory. Such a memory is something that orders living-toward the flourishing of hope rather than as contributing to destructive performances of exclusion and death through the commodification of life. In this analysis, 1 Corinthians 11 becomes a particularly important text since it can shape a eucharistic temporality that subverts the theocidal conditioning of the economization of global existence.

It is worth providing something of a set of readers' health warnings: the topic is a complex one, and the theorists engaged in this study are themselves producers of dense academic writing. The book has chosen not to soften the impact of this type of difficulty so as not to miss the depth of the subtleties required for understanding what is at issue, and therefore problematically provide a mollifying ease that dulls the intellect. Instead, readers are invited to work, to participate in the effort of intensive critical reflection, argument, and judgment regarding appropriate forms of action. The book does at least attempt to "translate" technical terms where it is feasible to do so. On the other hand, given the distinctly limited space the text is afforded, plenty of allusive moments have been retained as intellectual shorthand.

1

Ending as Arriving

"The End of History" and the Way to the Global Promised Land, or the Intensification of the Temporal Moment

According to Ulrich Beck: "Where there is no escape, people ultimately no longer want to think about it. This eschatological ecofatalism allows the pendulum of private and political moods to swing in *any* direction."[1] Where Beck announces a sense of entrapment

1. Ulrich Beck, *Risk Society: Towards a New Modernity* (London: Sage, 1992), 37.

that produces despair, Nicholas Lash recognizes (when pursuing reflections on the difficulty of meaningfully generating a critical hope) that not all the voices of the late twentieth century have been so despondent.[2] For instance, with the tearing down of the Berlin Wall in 1989, and the impending collapse of Soviet Communism and the Cold War, Francis Fukuyama in "triumphalistic notes" confidently announced "the end of history."[3] Strangely this was misunderstood by several critics as referring to some kind of ending of the temporal process itself.[4] One does not have to look far to see an explicit admission of his philosophical Hegelianism, with its immanentist providentialist eschatology. So he claimed that what has come to an end is "History: that is, history understood as a single, coherent, evolutionary process."[5] Modernity's historical trajectory has somewhat come to its ideological, if not yet its practical, *telos* in the "globalism" that is constituted by "the universalization of Western liberal democracy as the final form of human government."[6] All major conflicts at the level of political theory in the dialec-

2. Nicholas Lash, "Beyond the End of History?," *Concilium* 5 (1994): 47–56.
3. Citation from Graham Ward, *The Politics of Discipleship: Becoming Postmaterialistic Citizens* (Grand Rapids: Baker Academic, 2009), 59.
4. Francis Fukuyama addresses this misunderstanding in "The End of History: By Way of an Introduction" (1992), www.csf.colorado.edu/mirrors/ma...t/philosophy/works/us/fukuyama.htm.
5. Francis Fukuyama, *The End of History and the Last Man* (New York: Free Press, 2006), xii.
6. Francis Fukuyama, "The End of History?," *The National Interest* (Summer 1989): 3–18, https://tinyurl.com/y79upz99.

tical play of contradictions had been subverted since "the ideal of liberal democracy" cannot "be improved on."[7] Accordingly, any remaining problems in global geopolitical, social, and economic conditions were to be understood as "ones of incomplete implementation of the twin principles of liberty and equality on which modern democracy is founded, rather than of flaws in the principles themselves."

Practices Out of Time

A sense of the present as, in a somewhat different but overlapping sense, ending history can be accentuated through David Harvey's image of the telescoping compression of space and time. Living in this world entails that we have a certain circumscribed geography and temporal coordination, the manner of which has been reconfigured by technologies and by the market economy.[8] Closed borders are transgressed by the rapidity and consequent independencies of the deregulated and uncontrollable global financial flow, in what Anthony Giddens names their "butterfly effect," and are therein shrunk into what Marshall McLuhan describes as the "global village" of global interdependence.[9]

7. Fukuyama, *The End of History and the Last Man*, xi.
8. On the politico-economic consequences of the technological revolution see Manual Castells, *The Rise of the Network Society*, 2nd ed. (Oxford: Blackwell, 2000).

Mass television ownership, telecommunication systems, and internet usage, Harvey argues, collapse "the world's spaces" into a rush of simultaneous images.[10] A certain instantaneous multilocality, or border-transgressing omnipresence, is herein performed, adverting to a new way of being as being temporally disembodied.[11] Even the rhythms of day and night are dislocated and refigured by technologies for the sake of the profitability of market exchanges. Shopping malls, for instance, are "designed as they are to eradicate the distinction between night and day. . . . Daylight is unimportant, the climate is controlled, and you can shop furiously at ten o'clock at night."[12] What this informs is not merely the development of new technologies but the very conditions for being in the world. So Giddens argues that "instantaneous electronic communication isn't just a way in which news or information is conveyed more quickly. Its existence alters the very texture of our lives, rich and poor alike. When the image of Nelson Mandela maybe is more

9. Anthony Giddens, *The Consequences of Modernity* (Stanford: Stanford University Press, 1990), 64; Marshall McLuhan, in *Explorations in Communication: An Anthology*, ed. Edmund Carpenter and Marshall McLuhan (Boston: Beacon, 1960).

10. David Harvey, *The Condition of Postmodernity: An Enquiry into the Origins of Cultural Change* (Oxford: Basil Blackwell, 1989), 293.

11. Zygmunt Bauman, *Globalization: The Human Consequences* (Cambridge: Polity, 1998), 20. Margaret Wertheim suggests an analogy in a Christian vision of "heaven" ("The Pearly Gates of Cyberspace," in *Architecture of Fear*, ed. Nan Elin [New York: Princeton Architectural Press, 1997], 296).

12. Paul Lakeland, *Postmodernity: Christian Identity in a Fragmented Age* (Minneapolis: Fortress Press, 1997), 4.

familiar to us than the face of our next door neighbour, something has changed in the nature of our everyday experience."[13] Giddens's claim would be more effective if it used the examples of Beyoncé or David Beckman, popular icons, rather than that of Mandela, although his argument nevertheless remains a good one.

Even the post-human bodies we inhabit can experience the resurrection life now, since bodies apparently can be made perfect in the *hic et nunc.*[14] Not merely in Hollywood is the plastic, but merely cosmetic, cult of freezing or prolongating youth cultivated.[15] A veritable distance from having to face death can be further purchased with payments for hospice care for the elderly. Alongside technological corporations, the growth industries are those of leisure and health, thriving in and themselves reinforming, in Graham Ward's terms, "a culture of seduction, a culture of euphoric grasping of the present in order to forget the present."[16] "Today the tendency is to blot out fragility and vulnerability, weakness, guilt and decay, suffering, ageing and dying as completely as possible. One event, one entertainment, one festival follows the next. It's enjoyable, and

13. Anthony Giddens, *Runaway World*, Reith Lectures (April 1999), https://tinyurl.com/yashp8ns.
14. The City of Angels, LA, is an advert for this. See Graham Ward, *Cities of God* (London: Routledge, 2000).
15. IVF treatment for "older" couples is an important medical response to cultural shifts.
16. Ward, *Cities of God*, 68. See Harvey, *The Condition of Postmodernity*, 285.

that's enough. That was fun! When shall we have the next one?"[17]

"Time horizons shorten," or are intensively telescoped into a series of nonextensive "nowism" of disconnected moments, or rather a series of maximal momentary/instantaneous episodic impacts. Accordingly, Harvey argues that "the present is all there is."[18] The future does not exist, or at least it does not regulate one's behavior, and the past is doomed to obsolescence.[19] In the "hurried culture" every type of thing, it would seem, is being compressed into the instant—"fast-food," electronic mail, TV remotes and multichannel digital facilities, cyberspace and the intensity of the "knowledge economy," global social networks, and so on. These instants are also disposable, except for a few recyclable items.[20] Fashions, rapidly becoming global and socially homogenizing in their appeal through advertising and association with desired affluence, have a decreasing "shelf-life," and

17. Hans Kessler, "Fulfilment—Experienced for a Moment Yet Painfully Lacking," in Maureen Junker-Kenny and Miklós Tomka, *Faith in a Society of Instant Gratification*, volume 4, Concilium (London: SCM, 1999), 101–12 (103).
18. Stephen Bertman, *Hyperculture: The Human Cost of Speed* (Westport, CT: Praeger, 1998), cited in Zygmunt Bauman, *Does Ethics Have a Chance in a Society of Consumers?* (Cambridge, MA: Harvard University Press, 2008), 172; Harvey, *The Condition of Postmodernity*, 240. Cf. Fredric Jameson, *The Seeds of Time* (New York: Columbia University Press, 1994), 70; David Lyon, *Jesus in Disneyland: Religion in Postmodern Times* (Cambridge: Polity, 2000), 12.
19. Helga Nowotny, *Time: The Modern and Postmodern Experience* (Cambridge: Polity, 1994), 11.
20. Citation from Bertman, *Hyperculture*, in Bauman, *Does Ethics Have a Chance in a World of Consumers?*, 172.

necessarily so since the closure of desire for "more" would be the suffocation of the consumerist market. Even problem solving is quick-fix—wonder diets without the rigorous graft of intense physical exertion; sound-bite politics and short-term "relevancy" rather than slow, deep, and well-reasoned thinking and educative communication by debate; frail and superficial relations and divorce, where there has even been a matrimonial commitment, rather than the painful exertion of discovering new ways of dealing with relation difficulty, and so on. Time is evacuated of meaningful successiveness in favor of a regulating short-termism.[21] With this move, Harvey argues, comes "a . . . loss of depth" as exhibited in a cultural "fixation with appearances, surfaces, and instant impacts that have no sustaining power over time."[22] Or as Zygmunt Bauman describes it, "The insubstantial, instantaneous time of the software world is also an inconsequential time. 'Instantaneity' means immediate, 'on-the-spot' fulfilment—but also immediate exhaustion and fading of interest," "rapid learning—and swift forgetting."[23] In the "tyranny of the moment," the damage to possibilities for cultivating healthy social relations is pronounced.[24]

21. See Zygmunt Bauman, *Consuming Life* (Cambridge: Polity, 2007), 31.
22. Harvey, *The Condition of Postmodernity*, 58.
23. Zygmunt Bauman, *Liquid Modernity* (Cambridge: Polity, 2000), 118; *Does Ethics Have a Chance in a World of Consumers?*, 146.
24. The phrase is taken from Thomas Hylland Eriksen, *Tyranny of the Moment: Fast and Slow Time in the Information Age* (London: Pluto, 2001), 3.

> When the employment of labour has become short term, having been stripped of firm (let alone guaranteed) prospects and therefore made episodic, and when virtually all rules concerning the game of promotions and dismissals have been scrapped or tend to be altered well before the game is over, there is little chance for mutual loyalty and commitment to sprout up and take root. Unlike in the times of long-term mutual dependency, there is hardly any stimulus to take a serious, let alone critical, interest in the wisdom of an arrangement which is bound to be transient anyway.[25]

A whole series of simulacra is cultivated as milieu of escape, fantasy, and distraction, whether that be the "mindless hedonism of capitalist consumerism," narcotically induced fantasy, or the voracious craving of instantaneous experiences, "The drug of [the] ever new" as the deflation of boredom and prevention of stagnation.[26] This is why Bauman speaks of consumers as primarily accumulators of "the excitement of . . . new and unprecedented" *sensations* rather than of tangible possessions. William Cavanaugh has missed the nature of this consumptive experience of intangibles such as leisure when he claims that "shopping, not buying itself, is the heart of consumerism."[27] What occurs is that consumers live as if "acts of consumption

25. Zygmunt Bauman, *The Individualized Society* (Cambridge: Polity, 2001), 24.
26. Citations from Harvey, *The Condition of Postmodernity*, 60; Graham Ward, "Introduction, or, a Guide to Theological Thinking in Cyberspace," in *The Postmodern God: A Theological Reader*, ed. Graham Ward (Oxford: Blackwell, 1997), xv–xlvii (xv).

are seriously consequential for the authenticity of the self."[28] Don Slater refers to the substance of marketing strategies that fashion their message around products being "always improved and improving."[29] Likewise, Bauman connects fashion's self-promotion to the image of progress that "denigrates, in other words devalues, everything it leaves behind and replaces with something new."[30] This, however, is a somewhat misleading description since the notion of improvement or progress requires a temporal reference to what appeared previously, that which has been improved on. It would be better to speak of novelty in terms of a form of presentedness that is always new, and therefore episodic, momentary, temporally fragmented in an all-consuming present and intensive unification of global spaces into the interdependently metonymous "here."

Disciplined Commodification

What is presented is the consumer culture. Such a depiction of matters in terms of *culture* here, or the

27. William T. Cavanaugh, *Being Consumed: Economics and Christian Desire* (Grand Rapids: Eerdmans, 2008), 47.
28. Bauman, *Globalization*, 83; Don Slater, *Consumer Culture and Modernity* (Cambridge: Polity, 1997), 16.
29. Slater, *Consumer Culture and Modernity*, 10. Discourse of "authenticity," however, requires substantial articulation and critique, especially since Charles Taylor regards it as bound to an individualized subjectivity (*Philosophical Arguments* [Cambridge, MA: Harvard University Press, 1995], 227).
30. Bauman, *Culture in a Liquid Modern World*, 23.

biopolitical, serves to indicate the formative significance of the market.[31] As Athena Athanasiou catchily puts it, "there is nothing merely economic about economics."[32] What she has in mind is the *marketization*, *commodification*, and *aestheticization* of life. In fact, all of life is contained, embraced, and subjected so that nothing remains exempt from the market's discipline, the discipline of time itself. So Michael Hardt and Antonio Negri maintain that "Empire exhausts historical time, suspends history, and summons the past and future within its own ethical order. In other words, Empire presents its order as permanent, eternal, and necessary."[33] This is a global disciplining they regard as always having been in capital's sights, even though it has only been in the second half of the twentieth century that multi- or transnational industrial and financial corporations have begun to structure their activities around the biopolitical.[34] In consequence, now "they directly structure and articulate territories and populations."

Such a perspective had been somewhat anticipated some decades earlier by Karl Polanyi. For him the

31. The image of "biopolitics" was made famous by Michel Foucault, and Michael Hardt and Antonio Negri describe "biopolitical production" as "the production of social life itself, in which the economic, the political, and the cultural increasingly overlap and invest one another" (*Empire* [Cambridge, MA: Harvard University Press, 2000], xiii).

32. Athena Athanasiou, in Judith Butler and Athena Athanasiou, *Dispossession: The Performative in the Political* (Cambridge: Polity, 2013), 39.

33. Hardt and Negri, *Empire*, 11.

34. Hardt and Negri, *Empire*, 31.

period 1870–1914 was the first wave of a truly global capitalism, and the first step toward imposing a market logic on a range of human activities.[35] This involves society becoming "an adjunct to the market. Instead of the economy being embedded in social relations, social relations are embedded in the economic system."[36] The result of this process Slater articulates clearly: "Consumer culture denotes a social arrangement in which the relation between lived culture and social resources, between meaningful ways of life and the symbolic and material resources on which they depend, is mediated through markets."[37] The all-embracing range of the disciplining, what Hardt and Negri refer to as decentered and deterritorializing "empire" or "the sovereign power that governs the world," is relatively recent. It is the product of decisions made in the 1980s through Margaret Thatcher, Ronald Reagan, and Deng Xiaoping.[38] While these political choices have their roots in the liberal economy, Hardt and Negri argue that "imperial sovereignty marks a paradigm shift," a redistribution of power through the slippage of capital from statist hold.[39] Such economico-political decisions, what Harvey deems to

35. See Tony Schirato and Jen Web, *Understanding Globalization* (London: Sage, 2003), 88; Immanuel Wallerstein, *Geopolitics and Geoculture* (Cambridge: Cambridge University Press, 1991), 23.
36. Karl Polanyi, *The Great Transformation* (Boston: Beacon, 1957), 57, cited in Schirato and Web, *Understanding Globalization*, 88.
37. Slater, *Consumer Culture and Modernity*, 8.
38. Hardt and Negri, *Empire*, xi.
39. Hardt and Negri, *Empire*, 8.

be "a revolutionary turning-point in the world's social and economic history," have remade "the world around us in a totally different image."[40] The image, Harvey continues, is that of neoliberal economics and management: "Neoliberalism is in the first instance a theory of political economic practices that proposes that human well-being can best be advanced by liberating individual entrepreneurial freedoms and skills within an institutional framework characterized by strong private property rights, free markets, and free trade."[41] What was "heralded" herein, according to Slater, was "the subordination of production to consumption in the form of marketing: design, retailing, advertising and the product were ascendant, reflected in postmodern theory as the triumph of the sign and the aestheticization of everyday life."[42]

Appearance-Productivity

Slater alludes here to Jean Baudrillard's *Simulacra and Simulation*. Images, the surfaces exposed to instant perception, become more important than things in themselves, expressing a supposed distinctiveness of identity, and this sensibility has encouraged the recent explosion of image consultancies, the preeminence of

40. David Harvey, *A Brief History of Neoliberalism* (Oxford: Oxford University Press, 2005), 1.
41. Harvey, *A Brief History of Neoliberalism*, 2.
42. Slater, *Consumer Culture and Modernity*, 10.

brand logos, and the commodified insubstantiality of all things.[43] For Baudrillard, consumer society is driven by the excess of "a virtually unlimited productivity" more than the desires of consumers.[44] This entails that *disposability* more than productivity lie at the heart of the system of production, as does the manufacturing of consumptive consent that is required in order to dispose of products and generate wealth. Even for those less enamored by the culture of waste, the "spend-not-mend" sensibility, their purchases, especially of new technological devices, are necessarily subject to short-termism of planned or "built-in obsolescence." So, Baudrillard continues, "It becomes vital for the system at this stage to control not only the mechanism of production, but also consumer demand." Consequently, what predominates is a cultural ethos that puts a price on everything but can value nothing. It is economization or commodification without exception as the consumable of sheer will or desire. Therefore, continues Slater, "If there is no principle restricting who can consume what, there is also no principled constraint on *what* can be consumed: all social relations, activities

43. See Lyon, *Jesus in Disneyland*, 125. Thorstein Veblen sees consumer goods as markers of social prestige and status (*The Theory of the Leisure Class* [London: Constable, 1994]). In addition to Baudrillard's account of imagism one could profitably consider Guy Debord's analysis of the "society of the spectacle" (*The Society of the Spectacle* [Detroit: Black and Red, 1970]).
44. Jean Baudrillard, *Jean Baudrillard: Selected Writings*, ed. M. Poster (Stanford: Stanford University Press, 2001), 41. See Trevor Norris, "Hannah Arendt and Jean Baudrillard: Pedagogy in the Consumer Society," *Studies in Philosophy and Education* 25 (2006): 457–77.

and objects can in principle be exchanged as commodities. This is one of the most profound secularizations enacted by the modern world."[45]

Even ethics slides into liquidity and the "virtual reality" of "pop" aesthetics and fashionable forms of "relevance," with issues such as fur wearing, vegetarianism, sexual preferences, environmental degradation, and so on being presented forcefully only momentarily, and becoming victim to subsequent taste reversal. Nonetheless, the overwhelming individualization and aestheticization of the moral life reduces responsibility to the individuated subject.

> The concepts of responsibility and responsible choice, which resided before in the semantic field of ethical duty and moral concern for the Other, have shifted or have been moved to the realm of self-fulfilment and the calculation of risks. . . . "Responsibility" now means, first and last, *responsibility to oneself* ("you owe this to yourself," "you deserve it," as the traders in "relief from responsibility" put it), while "responsible choices" are, first and last, those moves serving the interests and satisfying the desires of the self. . . . The collateral victim of the leap to the consumerist rendition of freedom is the Other as object of ethical responsibility and moral concern.[46]

45. Slater, *Consumer Culture and Modernity*, 27.
46. Bauman, *Consuming Life*, 92.

So-called "religion" is likewise far from exempt from the effects of marketization and commodification. Vincent Miller, for instance, claims that the commodifying process results in a situation in which "elements of religious traditions are fragmented into discrete, free-floating signifiers abstracted from their interconnections with other doctrines, symbols, and practices. . . . Deprived of their coherence with a broader network of beliefs, they are more readily put to other uses, as shallow signifiers of whatever religious sentiment we desire."[47] Harvey Cox claims that this does not involve the "resacralization" of the Western world, or the return of the religions in a moment of desecularization, so much as "a fascinating *transformation of religion*, a creative series of self-adaptations by religions to the new conditions created by the modernity some of them helped to spawn."[48] In more extreme versions of this commodifying sensibility, religiosity becomes "soft," fluid, and inseparably bound to therapeutic forms of self-sculpting that suit narcissistic spiritual tastes and to entertainment value and affectivity.[49]

47. Vincent J. Miller, *Consuming Religion: Christian Faith and Practice in a Consumer Culture* (New York: Continuum, 2005), 3.
48. Harvey Cox, "The Myth of the Twentieth Century: The Rise and Fall of 'Secularization,'" in *The Twentieth Century: A Theological Overview*, ed. Gregory Baum (Maryknoll, NY: Orbis, 1999), 135–43 (139).
49. Ward, *The Politics of Discipleship*, 157. Citation from Graham Ward, "Religion After Democracy," in *After Modernity? Secularity, Globalization and the Re-Enchantment of the World*, ed. James K. A. Smith (Waco, TX: Baylor University Press, 2008), 203–17 (210). Ward calls commodified religion a "special effect" that offers an illusion of transcendence, and thus a simulation of religion.

This Ward describes as "eclectic customized spiritualities. . . . Postmodernity's religion is softer, more fluid, evasive, playful, narcissistic—closer to New Age spirituality, Gaia worship, Scientology, religions outside traditional frameworks. It . . . [is] more related to the spiritualizing of human subjectivity."[50] This welter of options "concentrates on religious function and tends towards privatization," ahistoricality, interiorization, frequently otherworldliness, and submission to the political and the cultural status quo.[51] Much of the spirituality or religiosity in the West today largely takes place outside of religious institutions and is consumerist in spirit—it involves an eclectic blend of religious stories and practices, constructed around the individual's needs or desires for satisfaction, or for the soothing of a beleaguered soul. "What we are witnessing is not a return [of religion] but a new religiousness that is hybrid, fluid, and commercialized."[52] Such a customized and bourgeois form of religiosity is a "liquid" spirituality customized for a lifestyle role for those accustomed to choosing their leisure and entertainment. So Ingolf Dalferth speaks of "cafeteria religion" as a way of depicting currents that encapsulate the value of choice and self-interest within religiosity—not merely the choice between different options of traditions, but between different elements of those tradi-

50. Ward, *The Politics of Discipleship*, 153.
51. Bauman, *Globalization*, 18. However, see Beyer, 3.
52. Ward, *The Politics of Discipleship*, 131.

tions.[53] Perhaps a better image would be that of "fusion religiosity" akin to "fusion cuisine" in terms of its eclecticism, or even "just-add-water spiritualities" in terms of its narratively undemanding instantaneity. Either way, the spiritual or the religious becomes something politically or publicly trivial. Therefore, this "religious" option fails to "redeem the secular. . . . [It] just leave[s] the secular to rot, retreating into privatised communities."[54]

It is clear, then, that the revolutionary impulses unleashed by policy decisions undertaken over the past three decades overflow the boundaries of economic practice and management to the point that they pervade the very way life is globally understood and lived, and considerably contribute to the setting of the terms within which "identity" and desire are disciplined (all the while imagining that we are "free," "free to choose").[55] Duncan Forrester accordingly observes that "market forces and market values have invaded one area after another, replacing existing values and procedures with market values and procedures."[56] "In

53. Ingolf U. Dalferth, "'I Determine What God Is!' Theology in the Age of 'Cafeteria Religion,'" *Theology Today* 57 (2000): 5–23.

54. Graham Ward, *Cities of God* (London: Routledge, 2000), 69. Cf. Miller, 177.

55. See Harvey, *A Brief History of Neoliberalism*, 3.

56. Duncan B. Forrester, *Christian Justice and Public Policy* (Cambridge: Cambridge University Press, 1997), 160. This echoes Karl Marx's observation in *The Communist Manifesto* about the capture of labor within a capitalist system: "The bourgeoisie has left no bond standing between one human being and another but naked interest, unfeeling 'cash payment.' . . . It has transformed the doctor, the lawyer, the cleric, the poet, the man of science into its paid labourers" (cited in Boyle, *Who Are We Now?*, 65).

some cases this has been extremely harmful," he continues, "because market forces can be destructive in dominant spheres of life in which they do not properly belong." One of the sets of ways in which this has been felt is in terms of the commodification of healthcare:

> When the market colonises the health care system, patients can become customers, symptoms rather than people are treated, there is an emphasis on productivity rather than care, the system becomes increasingly adversarial—patient and doctor seeing one another as potential opponents in court, and the practice of medicine is seen as a *battle* against disease, in which defeat is unthinkable, rather than the care of a sick person. Medical care is commodified and becomes enormously expensive.[57]

The Culture of Education's Marketization

Almost three decades ago, Neil Postman appealed to Cicero to articulate his understanding of education: "the purpose of education is to free the student from the tyranny of the present."[58] Yet within the reconfigured time of the neoliberalized market, the nature of the discipline provided by educational institutions is also concomitantly reconfigured in a form of training more appropriately arranged for the shifting polit-

57. Forrester, *Christian Justice and Public Policy*, 161.
58. Neil Postman, *Conscientious Objections: Stirring Up Trouble about Language, Technology, and Education* (New York: Vintage, 1992), 22.

ical conditions. Performance measures, KPIs (Key Performance Indicators), have been applied, or rather imposed on academics from above as Richard H. Roberts bemoaned a decade and a half ago.[59] Academics, reconstrued under this disciplinary regime, become pawns in political maneuvers driven preeminently by efficiency (read "the need to save public money") and market value (read "value for money"). That, of course, assumes there are full-time academics left to be measured in this way. It is unsurprising, then, that state-funded higher educational providers have been "encouraged" to court private industry investment and support, that students have become referred to preeminently as educational consumers, and that the *telos* of education is the training of students in skills for industry. Accordingly, the study grant support of studentships from the public purse has given way to loan schemes, self-funding, and the increasing need for part-time employment so that the economic form of "the biopolitics of social Darwinism" takes shape in terms of the survival of the richest, precisely what Thomas Henry Huxley had in mind when reconceiving Darwin's account of species mutation for American business interests.[60] As Brown argues, "Neoliberalism thus does not merely privatize—turn over to the

59. Richard H. Roberts, *Religion, Theology and the Human Sciences* (Cambridge: Cambridge University Press, 2002).
60. Athena Athanasiou, in Judith Butler and Athena Athanasiou, *Dispossession: The Performative in the Political* (Cambridge: Polity, 2013).

market for individual production and consumption—what was formerly publicly supported and valued. Rather, it formulates everything, everywhere, in terms of capital investment and appreciation, including and especially humans themselves."[61]

The title of a book in which Brown subjects the neoliberalizing of the university to exacting critique is hauntingly *Undoing the Demos*. The making of docile bodies ordered by the market, or as providing the "governing rationality," is rendering the universities a threat to the very idea and practices of participative democracy.[62] As cultural and educational theorist Henry Giroux argues, in the increasing normalization of the corporatized university in the late modern economy, "educational leadership is stripped of its ethical and political obligations and is redefined primarily as a matter of management, efficiency and cost-effectiveness."[63] The Humanities are reduced to, at best, romanticized versions of the self's interest or "taste," a reduction from humanization to an aesthetic couching of contemporary relevance. Here the aesthetic mode is construed apart from noetic and ethical value, and when the Humanities are spoken of in terms of "values education" they are so in rather vague ways that are materially light and undisruptive of not only

61. Wendy Brown, *Undoing the Demos: Neoliberalism's Stealth Revolution* (New York: Zone Books, 2015), 176.
62. Citation from Brown, *Undoing the Demos*, 176.
63. Henry Giroux, *Public Spaces, Private Lives: Beyond the Culture of Cynicism* (Lanham, MD: Rowman & Littlefield, 2002), 7.

the educativeness of scientific endeavors but the reduction of knowledge and thought to training. "The saturation of higher education by market rationality has converted higher education from a social and public good to a personal investment in individual futures, futures constructed mainly in terms of earning capacity."[64] After all, Brown observes, "Democracies are [now re]conceived as requiring technically skilled human capital, not educated participants in public life and common rule."[65] Moreover, that subject is not merely technically skilled, but irreducibly *competitive* (meaning not only enhancing the excellence of performance, but as inherently *agonistic*) and *self-interested.* And the universities are not contexts for the cooperatively productive pursuit of knowledge and mutually critically testable claims to the production of knowledge but are rather business ventures concerned for their own survival, productivity, profitability, and global reputation. Crucial to this is the research income and marketable prestige factors of high placings in the global competitive rankings, and the cost-saving efficiency strategies that tend toward replacing academic staff with cheap casual labor. Consequently, there is both a separation of research from teaching, with pure peer-to-peer research being devoid of public knowledge relevance either; and a degrading of the value of teaching while offering the

64. Brown, *Undoing the Demos*, 181.
65. Brown, *Undoing the Demos*, 177.

illusion of student input through consumer/student satisfaction surveys that orient student attitudes toward a "return on investment, whether in the form of entertainment or the enhancement of human capital."[66] Zygmunt Bauman and Leonidas Donskis rhetorically ask, "How will we form the next generation of . . . intellectuals and politicians if young people never have an opportunity to experience what a non-vulgar, non-pragmatic, non-instrumentalized university is like?"[67]

There is a certain irony, too, in the fact that religious, national/historical traditions are often preserved by being romanticized, commodified, and marketed, in what amounts to a Hollywoodization of our memories and a Bravehearting of nationalisms. What emerges from this form is a revisionist and nostalgic repackaging of the to-be-remembered past for the consumer age, a sort of sanitized selective amnesia, within the virtual narratives in which our lives may be situated.[68] And this is in spite of the fact that nation-states and local forms of government have become largely toothless pawns of a *global* disciplinary system, liquidated under the corrosive fluidity of capital and culture.[69] Nationalistic jingoism intensifies as a poten-

66. Brown, *Undoing the Demos*, 197.
67. Leonidas Donskis, in Zygmunt Bauman and Leonidas Donskis, *Moral Blindness: The Loss of Sensitivity in Liquid Modernity* (Cambridge: Polity, 2013), 139.
68. See Harvey, *The Condition of Postmodernity*, 303.
69. See Zygmunt Bauman and Carlo Bordoni, *State of Crisis* (Cambridge: Polity, 2014), 15; Nicholas Boyle, *Who Are We Now? Christian Humanism and the Global Market from Hegel to Heaney* (Notre Dame: University of Notre Dame Press, 1998), 37.

tial guarantee of self-securing at times of perceived crisis of identity or personal identification, and the fears generated over access to various sources of well-being such as economic stability that intensify a survivalist sensibility incompatible with any form of global identity and global range of responsibility.[70] As Hardt and Negri lament, "Fear is the ultimate guarantee of the new segmentations."[71] Yet, while nations continue to pretend to be the preeminent source of identification, meaning, and sustenance, the fact is that global networks and dependence exercise a more substantive disciplinarity.[72]

This is the context for the late-capitalist globalized self or subject-as-consumer, described by Cavanaugh through Fredric Jameson and Jacques Lacan as "schizophrenic," experiencing "only 'a series of pure and unrelated presents in time.'"[73] The temporality of becoming as a being-for-others is being displaced and the "social landscape of human life" is replaced by the increasingly atomized being as being-to-consume each present for oneself and then dispose of it in the next

70. See Bauman, *Strangers at Our Door*, 63, citing Eric Hobsbawm; Boyle, *Who Are We Now?*, 55, 76.
71. Hardt and Negri, *Empire*, 339. On fear as a weapon for government's making for a docile population in Hobbes, see 323.
72. This is a point made by Nicholas Boyle, *2014: How to Survive the Next World Crisis* (London: Continuum, 2010), 43.
73. William T. Cavanaugh, "The World in a Wafer: A Geography of the Eucharist as Resistance to Globalization," *Modern Theology* 15 (1999): 181–96 (188). Cf. Fredric Jameson, *Postmodernism, or, the Cultural Logic of Late Capitalism* (Durham, NC: Duke University Press, 1991), 27, xii.

present moment. As Bauman indicates, "Not togetherness, but avoidance and separation have become major survival strategies in the contemporary megalopolis."[74] While this is experienced as liberating by some, it is suffered as enslaving by others as their time of loss.[75] Michael Walzer for one regards the intensive individuation as a threat to both cooperative arrangements of cultural groups and democratic union.[76]

Therefore, it appears somewhat disingenuous for Fukuyama to echo what he describes from Hegel and Marx as a form of human society "that satisfied its deepest and most fundamental longings."[77] For as Bauman more accurately suggests, consumers' traveling is one "which makes arriving into a curse" for the sake of their continuing consuming.[78] This provides a taking "the waiting out of wanting," a side effect of which is the further compression of temporal horizons, a forgetting of the recently consumed by the artificially created pedagogy of the impetuous and pathological desire for the novel.[79] And yet there is something paradoxical about this display of eschatological instantaneity. Consumerism, the usually unquestioned ide-

74. Bauman, *Globalization*, 48.
75. Manfred B. Steger, *Globalization: A Very Short Introduction* (Oxford: Oxford University Press, 2003), 12.
76. Michael Walzer, *Citizenship and Civil Society* (Rutgers, NJ: New Jersey Committee for the Humanities Series on the Culture of Community, 1992), 11. Cf. Hardt and Negri, *Empire*, 399.
77. Fukuyama, "The End of History: By Way of an Introduction."
78. Bauman, *Globalization*, 83.
79. Bauman, *Globalization*, 79.

ological "ism" lying behind the consumer societies/cultures/ways of life of late- or postmodernity, what Steven Miles calls the dominant "religion" of the day, defers realization endlessly.[80] Salvation is given in and through the movement of consuming , and yet satisfaction is, in an important sense, never realized or realizable. Furthermore, and darker still, "to avoid frustration one had better refrain from developing habits and attachments or entering lasting commitments. The objects of desire are better enjoyed on the spot and then disposed of; markets see to it that they are made in such a way that both the gratification and the obsoleteness are instant."[81]

Market, How Free Are You?

Bauman's comments here suggest that there is a certain irony involved in using the term "*free*" of markets, since they provide not even so much what people want, never mind need, as what people will want and think they need. He speaks of seduction that cleverly leads us to imagine that in acting we are "in command."[82] Or as Nicholas Boyle observes, "Part of the

80. Steven Miles, *Consumerism—As a Way of Life* (London: Sage, 1998), 1. Cf. Colin Campbell, "I Shop Therefore I Know That I Am: The Metaphysical Basis of Modern Consumerism," in *Elusive Consumption*, ed. Karin M. Ekström and Helene Brembeck (Oxford: Berg, 2004).
81. Zygmunt Bauman, *The Individualized Society* (Cambridge: Polity, 2001), 156. Bauman suggests that this creates problems for the breakdown in human bonds.

appeal of a consumerist ideology is that it can appear to be radically opposed to coercion: if only people can be left free to pursue their desires, everyone will in the end have all that they want. The market, after all, has no powers of coercion: all its transactions are voluntary acts of exchange, and what is called is 'market discipline' is simply the process of adjustment by which sellers learn to be realistic about the strength of each other's desires."[83] One therefore has to attend to what Harvey lamentingly speaks of as marketing's "manipulating desires and tastes," and argues that the neoliberalization of capital has politically "become hegemonic as a mode of discourse."[84] This suggests a manner of being consumed by one's consumption, being compelled to act as consumers in response to the manufacturing and disciplining of consumer desire. What numerous critics observe, then, is the way that talk of freedom, whether that be related to choice or to desire itself, masks a docility produced by a systematic disciplining of choice and desire. In other words, given the way the market contributes to the generation and regulation of desire, it is dishonest to announce that the market *merely provides for*, and *responds to*, consumers' tastes and wants. Several critics understand this to be a deliberate move in terms of something like a "divide

82. Zygmunt Bauman, *Work, Consumerism and the New Poor* (Buckingham, UK: Open University Press, 1998), 26.
83. Boyle, *Who Are We Now?*, 44.
84. Harvey, *The Condition of Postmodernity*, 287; *A Brief History of Neoliberalism*, 3. Cf. 102; Miles, *Consumerism*, 50.

and conquer" economico-political sensibility. Consequently, Judith Butler for one can use a belligerent image when claiming that "there is a war on the idea of interdependency, . . . the social network of hands that seek to minimize the unlivability of lives."[85] We will have cause later to develop this notion of the precariousness of moral responsibility in the global market and the consumer culture it generates and sustains such that it entails justifications for making precarious the lives of others under the system. For now, the important point is the way that discourse of "freedom" proves to obfuscate cultural formations. Therefore, Peter Corrigan argues, "even the individuality of 'individual' taste may be an illusion in contemporary society."[86] The very terms by which consumers seek to give spontaneous expression are products of a whole host of factors, including the shaping of desires through encounters with others' desires, and therefore involve not only self-generated spontaneity of will but also a genealogically describable network of learnings.[87] Accordingly, Slavoj Žižek claims, "It is the ultimate irony of history that radical individualism serves as the ideological justification for the unconstrained power

85. Judith Butler, *Notes Toward a Performative Theory of Assembly* (Cambridge, MA: Harvard University Press, 2015), 67.
86. Peter Corrigan, *The Sociology of Consumption: An Introduction* (London: Sage, 1997), 120.
87. For a brief critique of moral construction based on an ethic of "choice" see Rowan Williams, "Making Moral Decisions," in *The Cambridge Companion to Christian Ethics*, ed. Robin Gill (Cambridge: Cambridge University Press, 2001), 3–15.

of what the large majority of individuals experience as a vast anonymous network that, without any democratic public control, regulates their lives."[88]

There is a second, and no less obfuscating difficulty that occurs with use of the term "free," and something that those who maintain that markets are morally neutral fail to acknowledge. That is the role of the state in opening and maintaining the markets. Before this observation can be made, something needs to be said about governmentality in globalized capital. Whereas Bauman regards this as a "*power free from politics*, and *politics devoid of power*," Hardt and Negri understand it not as a disappearance of the political but rather the disappearance of "any notion of the autonomy of the political," national sovereignty, since governmentality becomes shaped by capitalist corporate factors.[89] After all, "The development of the world market saps the foundations of nations as surely as of empires. From the point of view of the market, any act of national governance is a restrictive practice, an unwelcome form of protectionism, and national government itself, the raiser of taxes, the spender of other people's

88. Slavoj Žižek, *Against the Double Blackmail: Refugees, Terror and Other Troubles with the Neighbours* (London: Allen Lane, 2016), 57.
89. Zygmunt Bauman, *Collateral Damage: Social Inequalities in a Global Age* (Cambridge: Polity, 2011), 23; Hardt and Negri, *Empire*, 307. Cf. Brown, *Undoing the Demos*, 62. On the state's ongoing role of border-protection, see, e.g., Žižek, *Against the Double Blackmail*, 54; Luke Bretherton, "The Duty of Care to Refugees, Christian Cosmopolitanism, and the Hallowing of Bare Life," in *After Modernity? Secularity, Globalization and the Re-Enchantment of the World*, ed. James K. A. Smith (Waco, TX: Baylor University Press, 2008), 143–63.

money, the originator of regulations, the fixer of bank rates and would-be fixer of exchange rates, is just another vested interest, another unjustified obstacle to the free flow of capital.[90] Nations are growing obsolete, not as a matter of fashion or opinion, which could be altered by a determined personality, but as a result of an operation of the same economic trends that Thatcherism acknowledges and endorses."[91] Nonetheless, the governmentally minimalist nation-state remains crucial in some ways to the success of the neoliberalization of global economic life as guarantor of its operations, forcefully if required, and the provider of tax concessions on the flows of capital while maintaining necessary infrastructures through taxations on wages and salaries.[92] As Boyle maintains, "The more elaborate the system of exchange, and the more refined the arrangements for financing it, the greater is the need for a coercive power to audit, regulate, and protect it, and to resolve the multiplying conflicts within it—to define and defend property (real or intellectual) so that contracts may be made to convey it, to provide the courts where contractual disputes may be resolved, to settle a framework, which will eventually necessarily be international, within which conflicts of jurisdiction can be decided."[93] Fukuyama admits that

90. See Boyle, *2014*, 41.
91. Boyle, *Who Are We Now?*, 37.
92. See Harvey, *A Brief History of Neoliberalism*, 16.
93. Boyle, *Who Are We Now?*, 45.

"the United States and other democracies have a long-term interest in preserving the sphere of democracy in the world, and expanding it whenever possible and prudent."[94] This, along with the intensified policing of its borders, even comes through the state's violent flexing of its military muscle, one of its few tasks remaining with the deterritorialization of the power of capital. Consequently, if one were to contest Duncan Forrester's appeal, largely made in critical response to the work of Hayek, for intervention and regulation when asserting that "the market must be harnessed to serve the ends of justice," the response should include the recognition that the markets already bear the imprint of interventionist political agency.[95]

Following on from this set of themes is a third way in which talk of "freedom" is manifestly problematic, and this point will be unpacked a little more in the following chapter: "The free flow of capital to move around the globe does not mean that people can move about the globe to follow opportunities; it means that corporations are free to pursue their greatest profit, pretty much regardless of the human consequences and without regard to the social costs (and benefits of production)."[96]

Moreover, and fourthly, there is a significant issue with regard to the connection of rhetoric of freedom

94. Fukuyama, *The End of History*, 280.
95. Forrester, *Christian Justice and Public Policy*, 157.
96. Schirato and Webb, *Understanding Globalization*, 96.

and the exercise of power. A politics of freedom when construed as "freedom of choice" or "freedom not to be interfered with" not only lacks a substantive notion of the good, but operates from a sense of equitable access to resources. This assumption is particularly evident in the rhetoric of self-help therapies, and the anti-welfare sentiment that apportions blame on those who are unsuccessful. Yet as Harvey observes, even in terms of production, "Competition often results in monopoly or oligopoly, as stronger firms drive out weaker."[97] The consequences for the employment sector can be significant with the mobility of transnational corporations and industries being able to relocate while leaving its workers bereft of income by virtue of their inability to follow the move particularly when that shift crosses national borders. The redundant thereby lose access to the consumer market.

> It is precisely in the context of diminished personal resources derived from the job market that the neoliberal determination to transfer all responsibility for well-being back to the individual has doubly deleterious effects. As the state withdraws from welfare provision and diminishes its role in arenas such as health care, public education, and social services, which were once so fundamental to embedded liberalism, it leaves larger and larger segments of the population exposed to impoverishment. The social safety net is reduced to a bare minimum in favour of a system that emphasizes

97. Harvey, *A Brief History of Neoliberalism*, 67.

> personal responsibility. Personal failure is generally attributed to personal failings, and the victim is all too often blamed.[98]

That is not all. Harvey continues with what amounts to a fifth observation by relating how "the state typically produces legislation and regulatory frameworks that advantage corporations, and in some instances specific interests such as energy, pharmaceuticals, agribusiness, etc."[99] The process of corporate lobbying of government in the United States cannot be ignored in this context. Recourse to the legal system is itself very far from conducive to equity in this context since "the courts are in any case heavily biased towards ruling class interests, given the class allegiance of the judiciary," and the power of council that wealth generates.[100] "Legal decisions tend to favour rights of private property and the profit rate over rights of equality and social justice." Law is only as representative as the values and the power to maintain those values. The difficulty particularly comes when the law is demarcated from the governing value of justly serving the *common* good. "[L]aws without virtues can be only a source of disguised tyranny."[101]

98. Harvey, *A Brief History of Neoliberalism*, 76.
99. Harvey, *A Brief History of Neoliberalism*, 77.
100. Harvey, *A Brief History of Neoliberalism*, 177.
101. D. Stephen Long, *Divine Economy: Theology and the Market* (London: Routledge, 2000), 240.

Finally, "Within the world's dense network of global interdependence, we cannot be sure of our moral innocence whenever other human beings suffer indignity, misery, or pain."[102] Even the processes of production are shrouded in mysterious complexity, with outsourced labor at most points in the process. A claim by Cavanaugh is not unhelpful in opening up a few of the issues at stake in this regard:

> My exchange with the supermarket is less than free, because the information I need is not readily available to me. Before I read Michael Pollan, I had only the vaguest sense of how beef is typically raised. The ranchers and feedlot workers chafe under the compulsion of market forces beyond their control, and all the while their profit margins are squeezed even tighter by the four conglomerates that dominate the meatpacking industry. And the overall effect of the system on the environment and on rural communities has been devastating.[103]

102. Bauman, *Does Ethics Have a Chance in a World of Consumers?*, 72.
103. Cavanaugh, *Being Consumed*, 31.

2

Globalizing Waste

The Productivity of the Market

Fukuyama's neoliberal thesis is that while stable liberal democracies have not yet become universally politically available, philosophically "liberal democracy remains the only coherent political aspiration that spans different regions and cultures around the globe."[1] Of course, a Marxist should ask about the convenience of Fukuyama's historicist move from noting

1. Francis Fukuyama, "The End of History: By Way of an Introduction" (1992).

the collapse of Communism as governmental system to his assurance that Marx's economic and political theories have been "disproven."[2] Equally, one should be suspicious of the glib claim that human beings would be satisfied by liberal egalitarianism in politics, economics, and culture (what Fukuyama calls the desire for "universal and reciprocal recognition").[3] Moreover, questions have to be asked about the unacknowledged perspectivism attending his appreciation of Alexandre Kojève's grand Hegelian value-judgment on history's teleology (which is, in actuality, *engineered*) toward liberal democracy (and one that fragilely depends upon the pragmatics of majority consensus).[4] Thus, while Jean-François Lyotard has made famous the post–grand narrative claims of modernity for the fragmented consciousnesses of *The Postmodern Condition*, neoliberal narratives sound very grand and masterly indeed.[5] As Hardt and Negri argue, "the imperial machine, far from eliminating master narratives, actually produces them (ideological master narratives in

2. For such a reading of Fukuyama see Fadia Gharib, "Francis Fukuyama's The End of History and the Last Man: Another Interpretation" (Dec. 1997), www.yorku.ca/faculty/academic/fgharib/fukuyama.html.
3. Fukuyama, "The End of History."
4. Fukuyama, "The End of History." Manfred B. Steger claims that Fukuyama sounds like an American applying "the old theme of manifest destiny to the global arena" (*Globalization: A Very Short Introduction* [Oxford: Oxford University Press, 2003], 73).
5. William T. Cavanaugh, "The World in a Wafer: A Geography of the Eucharist as Resistance to Globalization," *Modern Theology* 15 (1999): 182. John Ralston Saul claims that this is "a type of religious fundamentalism" (*The Collapse of Global Capitalism* [London: Atlantic Books, 2005], 48).

particular) in order to validate and celebrate its own power."[6] Yet it offers the story as one of benign productivity, since "Empire is formed not on the basis of force itself but on the basis of the capacity to present force as being in the service of right and peace."[7]

Globalization, Homogenization, and Difference

Yet globalization's neoliberal "spin-doctors" advance that the process of globalization's globality does not flatten the time of what is different. Localities and cultures are self-protecting and self-sustaining, adding their own local flavors to the global marketplace, what Roland Robertson calls "glocalization."[8] Advertised is the fact that the success story of American fast food global companies, like McDonald's, has had to *give in to local tastes* by adding local variations to its menus in the Indian subcontinent. However, this "glocal" appeals more to rhetoric than reality. "The idea that such cultures may subtly differentiate themselves region by region, so that what we have is 'glocalism' rather than globalization is a fantasy dreamed up by advertising agents. Fast food is fast food and Coke is Coke. It is a

6. Michael Hardt and Antonio Negri, *Empire* (Cambridge, MA: Harvard University Press, 2000), 34.
7. Hardt and Negri, *Empire*, 15.
8. Roland Robertson, "Glocalization: Time-Space and Homogeneity-Heterogeneity," in *Global Modernities*, ed. Mike Featherstone, Scott Lash, and Roland Robertson (London: Sage, 1995), 25–44.

way of life that is sold, a new mutation on the imperial dream."[9]

Fukuyama, on the other hand, does admit to a certain homogenization of social tastes and values.[10] Nevertheless, this is carefully packaged within his celebration that "good news has come," "the gates of the Promised Land of liberal democracy" can be viewed and entered, and that rhetoric comes on the heels of late twentieth-century historical pessimism.[11] The free markets have successfully produced "unprecedented levels of material prosperity" in both industrially developed and developing countries, deeply and necessarily connected with "the move toward political freedom around the globe."[12] Globalization can peacefully negotiate, manage, and incorporate differences into its spreading catholicity while beneficently eradicating division. Cavanaugh observes that "the result" of this rhetoric is a mood that assumes "an eschatology in which abundance for all is just around the corner."[13]

9. Timothy Jarvis Gorringe, "Invoking: Globalization and Power," in *The Blackwell Companion to Christian Ethics*, ed. Stanley Hauerwas and Samuel Wells (Oxford: Blackwell, 2004), 346–59 (351).

10. George Ritzer famously spoke of *The McDonaldization of Society* (Thousand Oaks, CA: Pine Forge, 1993).

11. Louis Emmerij, "World Economic Changes at the Threshold of the Twenty-First Century," in *Global Futures: Shaping Globalization* (London: Zed Books, 2000), 53–62.

12. Fukuyama, "The End of History: By Way of an Introduction." Cf. R. Barnet and J. Cavanaugh, *Global Dreams: Imperial Corporations and the New World Order* (New York: Simon & Schuster, 1994); Friedrich A. Hayek, *The Road to Serfdom* (London: Routledge, 2001); Milton Friedman, *Capitalism and Freedom* (Chicago: University of Chicago Press, 1962).

An example of this occurs in a claim made several years ago by the then president of the Nabisco Corporation: "Utopia is One world of homogeneous consumption. . . . [I am] looking forward to the day when Arabs and Americans, Latins and Scandinavians will be munching Ritz crackers as enthusiastically as they already drink Coke or brush their teeth with Colgate."[14] Yet would this be peacefulness, or the banality of those apathetic to anything other than simulacra? The seduction of "bread and circuses" is, after all, an ancient and well-tried formula for social control.[15] Is consumerism not a pathetic reduction of the Enlightenment ideal of freedom to "a few trivial aesthetic choices, made from a range predetermined by [multinational] corporations"?[16] The flourishing of "a vigorous civil society" is being subverted—freedom is impoverished by being negatively reimagined as, at most, noninterference and therefore indifference to matters of difference.[17] The formal function of the democratic state may remain (for example, a choice

13. William T. Cavanaugh, *Being Consumed: Economics and Christian Desire* (Grand Rapids: Eerdmans, 2008), 93.
14. Cited in Cavanaugh, "The World in a Wafer," 185, repeating the citation by Jerry Mander, "The Rules of Corporate Behavior," in *The Case Against the Global Economy*, ed. Jerry Mander and Edward Goldsmith (San Francisco: Sierra Club, 1996), 321.
15. David Harvey, *A Brief History of Neoliberalism* (Oxford: Oxford University Press, 2005), 88.
16. Alan Aldridge, *Religion in the Contemporary World: A Sociological Interpretation* (Oxford: Polity, 2000), 190.
17. Graham Ward, *The Politics of Discipleship: Becoming Postmaterialistic Citizens* (Grand Rapids: Baker Academic, 2009), 113.

of candidates at the secret ballot) but possibilities for civic participation in political power is under erasure, and the citizen-subject is evisceratingly subjected to transfiguration into the consumer subject. Bauman, for instance, identifies and laments the contemporary privatization of dissent, expressed in public indifference or politically diluted single-issue campaigns, or "private escapes from public squalor."[18] At worst, Bauman detects the post-politicization of the cultural imagination in consumptive lifestyles. In such an account, Western societies are, in Neil Postman's striking phrase, "amusing ourselves to death" in their panopticonic docility, engaging, in Bauman's image, in "identainment."[19] The likes of Postman, Bauman, and Giroux, among others, then trace a particularly Huxleyan dystopian current in contemporaneity. In this vein it is arguable that "the leisure which was originally claimed under the impact of industrialisation in order to humanise the impact of meaningless toil becomes the ultimate instrument in our dehumanisation."[20]

18. Zygmunt Bauman, *Intimations of Postmodernity* (London: Routledge, 1992), 181. Moreover, as Cobb reflects, what constitutes "modest consumption" is defined by the market (John B. Cobb Jr., "Consumerism, Economism, and Christian Faith," *Religion Online* [2000], https://tinyurl.com/ycvt8vhb).
19. Neil Postman, *Amusing Ourselves to Death: Public Discourse in the Age of Show Business* (New York: Penguin, 1985); Bauman, in Zygmunt Bauman and Leonidas Donskis, *Moral Blindness: The Loss of Sensitivity in Liquid Modernity* (Cambridge: Polity, 2013), 33.
20. Timothy J. Gorringe, *Capital and the Kingdom: Theological Ethics and Economic Order* (Maryknoll, NY: Orbis, 1994), 71.

The dissolution of sustainable and rigorous political analysis and argument beyond the hegemonic marketization of values thereby makes careful analysis and rigorous public debate an impossibility. The market has proven itself to be sufficiently flexible to be able to absorb resistance into itself, and commodifyingly package and "sell the T-shirt" for things like anti-globalization campaigns. Accordingly, the capacity for failing to contest certain types of systemic violence becomes mitigated, subject to the rhetorical whims of governmentality's "spin doctors." As Carl Schmitt argued, "where there is no discussion there is dictatorship."[21] The significance of this incontestability, the inability to entertain any critical alternative, is hidden in perspectives that either understand the market as morally neutral or as providing an ending to history that embeds morally valuable democratic practices of contractually enforceable relations and egalitarian status before the law.

A Winning Accumulation by Dispossession

Yet, there is a substantial case to be made that "while Empire may have played a role in putting an end to colonialism and imperialism, it nonetheless constructs its own memberships of power based on exploitation that are in many respects more brutal than those it

21. Carl Schmitt, *Political Theology: Four Chapters on the Concept of Sovereignty*, trans. George Schwab (Cambridge, MA: MIT Press, 1985), 78.

destroyed."[22] The issue turns on a significant gap between neoliberal rhetoric and political reality, "a burgeoning disparity between the declared public aims of neoliberalism—the well-being of all—and its actual consequences—the restoration of class power."[23] In Harvey's analysis, the telltale sign is the fact that wealth is less being generated than *redistributed*, an "accumulation by dispossession."[24]

The very idea that this might be—just might be—the fundamental core of what neoliberalization has been about all along appears unthinkable. It has been part of the genius of neoliberal theory to provide a benevolent mask full of wonderful-sounding words like *freedom*, *liberty*, *choice*, and *rights*, to hide the grim realities of the restoration or reconstitution of naked class power, locally as well as transnationally, but most importantly in the main financial centers of global capitalism.[25]

The theme of regulative class power is developed by Hardt and Negri, who observe that "today nearly all of humanity is to some degree absorbed within or subordinated to the networks of capitalist exploitations."[26] This critical claim works itself out in a variety of ways, and it does so for Hardt and Negri in such a way as to

22. Hardt and Negri, *Empire*, 43.
23. Harvey, *A Brief History of Neoliberalism*, 79.
24. Harvey, *The New Imperialism* (Oxford: Oxford University Press, 2003), ch. 4.
25. Harvey, *A Brief History of Neoliberalism*, 119. Cf. Daniel M. Bell Jr., *The Economy of Desire: Christianity and Capitalism in a Postmodern World* (Grand Rapids: Baker, 2012), 60.
26. Hardt and Negri, *Empire*, 43.

entail that there can be no critical *repair* of "the contemporary configuration of capitalism." For them the dehumanizing damage runs through the system itself. Consequently, they maintain, "the core of capitalist reproduction and accumulation necessarily implies imperialist expansion" so that "the evils of imperialism cannot be confronted except by destroying capitalism itself."[27]

John Cobb, for instance, claims that far from achieving peacefulness, globalization actually increases social alienations and violence.[28] There are a number of ways in which such a claim can be articulated. For instance, competitive marketing strategies have brought localities into conflict with each other in the search for industry creation, fragmenting social orders into increasingly atomized individuals who are only bound to each other by the temporary contract, and have generated socially disruptive mobilities with the hypermobility of location and relocation.[29] According to Cavanaugh, "It is not simply that the market encourages an erotic attraction toward things and not persons . . . [but that it] establishes a fundamentally individualistic view of the human person."[30] "'I shop therefore I am.'"[31] This is not all, however. The individuated subject is construed competitively, as self-

27. Hardt and Negri, *Empire*, 228, 229.
28. Cobb, "Economism as Idolatry."
29. Cavanaugh, "The World in a Wafer," 186.
30. Cavanaugh, *Being Consumed*, 91.

interested and self-serving. There is something poignant, then, in Bauman's closing his 1998 study on globalization with a chapter on justice and on penal systems in global states. Security, professionalized as an activity that itself is commodified so as to shift into an industry that expensively sells "the safe environment," offers fortification against all uninviteds, with the secluding gating of "communities" from those who want what the self-securing have.[32] The parallel at a state level becomes the surveillance state's unrelenting policing of its borders lest the "illegal" or "redundant people" penetrate, or quelling dissent lest the disenfranchised demonstrate political resistance.[33] Borders may be porous to capital and the "knowledge economy" but their walls are not to be easily scaled by people, or at least not by those cast adrift from what the market deems to be market successes.

According to several critics, then, globalization is a religion only of the "winners."[34] And, indeed, it does have its own discourse of damnation concerning the losers, those, according to Bill Gates, who do not participate in world free trade.[35] Mahathir Mohammad,

31. Harvey, *A Brief History of Neoliberalism*, 170. Cf. Colin Campbell, "I Shop Therefore I Know That I Am," in *Elusive Consumption*, ed. Karin M. Ekström and Helen Brembeck (Oxford: Berg, 2004), 27–44.

32. See Bauman on the threats from within the cityscape (*Globalization*, 47).

33. Zygmunt Bauman, *Strangers at Our Door* (Cambridge: Polity, 2016), 3.

34. See, for example, Colin Hines, *Localization: A Global Manifesto* (London: Earthscan, 2000), viii.

35. At the World Economic Forum's Asia-Pacific summit in Melbourne (11–13 September 2000).

the Malaysian Prime Minister at the South Summit of the G77 (April 12, 2000), asserted that globalization has shown signs of becoming a religion that tolerates no heresy. This he felt was unfortunate since properly interpreted and regulated globalization can benefit both rich and poor.[36] Others, however, have been even more damning in their assessments, especially since this religion is showing signs of silencing, primarily through avoidance, any voices that express discontent. In such a reading Mahathir Mohammad's claim would be infected with a theodical legitimation of the market, rhetorically determining the perfecting of global processes and systems that are currently suffered by many within a sacrificial and futurist perfectionist logic that silences possibilities for resistance. Manuel Castells, in contrast, asserts that the free market is contributing to, rather than alleviating, poverty.[37] After all, the globalized markets, which are in any case extremely volatile in their dynamic, despite the rhetoric of beneficence, remain a profit-maximizing arrangement, and as such have a narrow and short-term view that incapacitates them from taking into account those who are not seen as profit material (including those who cannot be encouraged into live-long credit card debts).[38] "When the market

36. Mahathir Mohammad, www.twnside.org.sg/title/twr117e.htm, consulted 30-03-01.
37. Manuel Castells, cited in Agustí Nicolau and Manuel Manonelles, "Cultural Diversity and Globalisation," www.millenniumforum.org/html/docs/Cultural Diversity and Globalisation.htm, consulted 30-03-01.

mechanism becomes the sole arbiter of the desirable and the undesirable—a virtual source of values—the result is that ethical norms are gradually eroded and the dimensions of justice grossly violated."[39] According to Bauman in something of a sound-bite set of statements,

> All consumer goods, including those described as "durable," are eminently exchangeable and expendable. . . . A consumerist attitude may lubricate the wheels of the economy; [but] it sprinkles sand into the bearings of morality. . . . [T]he consumerist culture . . . transforms every shop and service agency into a pharmacy purveying tranquillizers and anaesthetic drugs: in this case drugs intended to mitigate or altogether placate *moral*, rather than physical pains.[40]

Consequently, while the post-statist fluidity of capital and its cultural effectiveness biopolitically is experienced as a boon for some, it is received as a considerable bane for many.[41] Yet these consequences, especially in terms of the conditions of the production of consumable items and experiences, are hidden in the invisibility of complex systems of productivity.

38. George Soros, "A Failed Philosopher Tries Again," Jan Patocka Memorial Lecture (1995), https://tinyurl.com/y827v45z.
39. Khurshid Ahmad, "The Challenge of Global Capitalism: An Islamic Perspective," in *Making Globalization Good: The Moral Challenges of Global Capitalism*, ed. John H. Dunning (Oxford: Oxford University Press, 2003), 181–209 (186).
40. Bauman, in Bauman and Donskis, *Moral Blindness*, 15.
41. So Bauman, *Globalization*, 2.

They are hidden, too, in the distraction of the consumer's gaze at herself and all that will enhance her consumption and waste disposal. Nonetheless, as Boyle argues, "We live in one world. The intellectual fashion for holding that we live in multiple, disconnected worlds is a device of consumerism to prevent us from recognizing our common fate, lest we are tempted to try to control it. . . . The unity of the human race may once have been only an idea: it is nowadays also material. We are all related to one another through the economic process of production and exchange (and so are coming to give real significance to our genetic unity)."[42]

At the very least, long-term sociocultural planning lies increasingly out of the reach of a considerable proportion of the global population, while larger amounts of wealth are being relocated in the hands of an economic elite. A globalizing marketplace, and that constructed with a hegemonic Western urban trajectory, needs to have no space or time for the poor, a poor who are further exploited into losing their own values in dreaming of the accumulation of Western urban lifestyles, and who are often required to cheaply oil the wheels of the various forms of the capitalist machine.[43]

42. Nicholas Boyle, *Who Are We Now? Christian Humanism and the Global Market from Hegel to Heaney* (Notre Dame: University of Notre Dame Press, 1998), 313.
43. On the implications of Adam Smith's economics for the slave trade, see D. Stephen Long, *Divine Economy: Theology and the Market* (London: Routledge, 2000), 104.

As Harvey maintains, "Under neoliberalization, the figure of 'the disposable worker' emerges as prototypical on the world stage."[44] If the market is morally neutral and moral responsibility is reduced to a private choice, then even to consider discussing practices of global capital exchange in the context of matters of justice would be a category mistake. Milton Friedman puts the matter particularly starkly:

"Few trends could so thoroughly undermine the very foundations of our free society as the acceptance by corporate officials of a social responsibility other than to make as much money for their stockholders as possible." This is a fundamentally subversive doctrine. If businessmen do have a social responsibility, other than making maximum profits for stockholders, how are they to know what it is? Can self-selected private individuals decide what the social interest is?[45]

Wastefully Desiring Defacement by Savage Capitalism

Such a claim lends considerable weight to Daniel M. Bell's use of Franz Hinkelammert's critique of "savage capitalism."[46] If the capital-regulating welfare state constitutes a version of "capitalism with a human

44. Harvey, *A Brief History of Neoliberalism*, 169. Harvey makes the case that it is particularly "women, for the most part, and sometimes children [who] bear the brunt" of the dark underside of the global market (170).
45. Milton Friedman, *Capitalism and Freedom* (Chicago: University of Chicago Press, 1962), 133.

face," the post-statist flows of economic power have unfettered capital in such a way that it can practice an appearance characterizable as an inhuman face. Capital, and its masters, operates in a *no-place*, a digital financialization that emancipates and immunizes it from not only the control of places of governance, but leaves it utterly unaccountable but for the regulating ideal of a pure "ethics for profit."[47]

This is precisely what critics such as Bauman resist on the basis of economic practices being practices of exchange *between people*, and configuring the very understanding of the agential *subject*. Accordingly, talk of moral neutrality either involves one of two things. Either it expresses a significant naïveté on the part of its proponents, especially since all practices embody sets of beliefs about human relations or people's relation to the world more generally, and enable "us to construe our lives . . . in terms of the activities of producers and consumers."[48] Or it functions to surreptitiously obfuscate for the purposes of ethico-political legitimation. Either way it rhetorically masks an ontology, an "ontological capture" in a manner that attempts to move beyond the dominance of Hobbesian and neo-Darwinian portrayals of human desire.[49] "By

46. Daniel M. Bell Jr., *Liberation Theology After the End of History: The Refusal to Cease Suffering* (London: Routledge, 2001), 10.
47. Carlo Bordoni, in Bauman and Bordoni, *State of Crisis*, 117.
48. Long, *Divine Economy*, 4.
49. Citation from Daniel M. Bell Jr., "Only Jesus Saves: Toward a Theopolitical Ontology of Judgment," in *Theology and the Political: The New Debate*, ed. Cre-

bracketing truth and goodness out of the picture, liberalism does not so much liberate society from the 'tyranny of the Good' as impose a new tyranny of freedom from any sense of mutual obligation, which paradoxically enslaves the supposedly emancipated subject."[50] Harvey, in fact, argues that the system is designed not to maximize profits in some globally distributive fashion, but to deliberatively enhance the power of the economically elite classes:

> We can, therefore, interpret neoliberalization either as a *utopian* project to realize a theoretical design for the reorganization of international capitalism or as a *political* project to re-establish the conditions for capital accumulation and to restore the power of economic elites. . . . Thirty years of neoliberal freedoms have, after all, not only restored power to a narrowly defined capitalist class. They have also produced immense concentrations of corporate power in energy, the media, pharmaceuticals, transportation, and even retailing (for example Wal-Mart). The freedom of the market that [George W.] Bush proclaims as the high point of human aspiration turns out to be nothing more than the convenient means to spread corporate monopoly power and Coca Cola everywhere without constraint. With disproportionate influence over the media and the political process this class (with Rupert Murdoch and Fox news

ston Davis, John Milbank, and Slavoj Žižek (Durham, NC: Duke University Press, 2005), 200–227 (200).

50. John Milbank and Adrian Pabst, *The Politics of Virtue: Post-Liberalism and the Human Future* (Lanham, MD: Rowman & Littlefield, 2016), 19.

> in the lead) has both the incentive and the power to persuade us that we are all better off under a neoliberal regime of freedoms.[51]

The narrative is always one of scarcity and anxiety over this scarcity that necessitates a push for further accumulation, growth, efficiency, and greater profit-margins. A CEO, for instance, would be swiftly replaced if she were to announce at the corporation's annual general meeting that "we made too much last year," or "the company has grown too powerful." In fact, argues Bauman, the tax cuts for corporations and the rich that are rhetorically legitimated with an appeal to "trickle-down economics" are themselves purposed "to *secure privileges*, not to harness them to public service."[52] "Its effect," he continues, "is the exemption of a narrow group of top earners from the impact of whatever calamity their activities might have visited on all those whose livelihood they've exposed to the vagaries of fate." Hardt and Negri agree with Harvey's analysis, and that of Fredric Jameson, for whom "the global politics of difference established by the world market is defined not by free play and equality, but by the imposition of new hierarchies, or really by a constant process of hierarchization."[53]

51. Harvey, *A Brief History of Neoliberalism*, 19, 38. Harvey speaks of elites rather than class, given the reconfigurations of power around financial gain and capital control (see 31).
52. Zygmunt Bauman, *Does the Richness of the Few Benefit Us All?* (Cambridge: Polity, 2013), 44.

One could at this point apply Terry Eagleton's use of the image of the vampire to the politico-economic conditions of the contemporary global market, "leeching life from others in order to fill an aching absence in oneself."[54] Or perhaps the metaphor of the demonic is more fitting: "They believe in power, appetite, self-interest, rational calculation, and nothing else."[55] This certainly captures the sheer will to financially acquire on the part of corporations and financial firms.[56] On the other hand, there is something equally poignant in Henry Giroux's development of the figure of the zombie to describe current configurations of power.[57] All these suggest that the systemic disciplinary co-option of instrumental rationality witnesses to intense patterns of destruction endemic to the very fabric of economico-political activities. This destructively instrumentalizing configuration of things and persons is such that it may take the very ecology of life past the point of no return for the livability of future generations.

Bauman describes conditions of intensifying poverty and rising inequality through several arresting euphemisms: as the reduction of persons to a

53. Hardt and Negri, *Empire*, 154.
54. Terry Eagleton, *On Evil* (New Haven: Yale University Press, 2010), 71.
55. Eagleton, *On Evil*, 75.
56. John Maynard Keynes regarded avarice as a vice (*Essays in Persuasion* [New York: W. W. Norton & Co., 1963], 358–73).
57. Henry A. Giroux, preface to *Zombie Politics and Culture in the Age of Casino Capitalism*, 2nd ed. (New York: Peter Lang, 2014).

"human waste disposal industry" and as the "'collateral damage' of global laissez-faire" or market forces.[58] The rhetorical impact of reducing people to such euphemistic description is itself a quite deliberate move on Bauman's part, and enables him to provide an ideology-exposing identification and critique of the erasing of human beings in and as the waste by-product of the processes of the global market. The political use of such euphemisms domesticates otherwise complex ways of making political judgments, and supervises the conditions for the formation of political sensibility so that they become, to draw on Foucault's language, "the means by which subjects of knowledge are formed, and hence are truth relations."[59] "Some lives are grievable," but their lives, dehumanized as they are by euphemistic reduction, are not.[60] As Bauman argues, "Being but a sideline of economic progress, the production of human waste has all the markings of an impersonal, purely technical issue. The principal actors in the drama are 'terms of trade,' market demands,' 'competitive pressures,' 'productivity' or 'efficiency' requirements, all covering up or explicitly denying any connection with the inten-

58. Zygmunt Bauman, *Wasted Lives: Modernity and Its Outcasts* (Cambridge: Polity, 2004), 6; *Collateral Damage: Social Inequalities in a Global Age* (Cambridge: Polity, 2011), 26.
59. Michel Foucault, *Power: Essential Works of Foucault 1954-1984*, ed. James D. Faubion (New York: New Press, 1994), 15.
60. Judith Butler, *Precarious Mourning: The Powers of Mourning and Violence* (London: Verso, 2004), xiv.

tions, will, decisions and actions of real humans with names and addresses."[61] It hardly needs to be said that talk of "efficiency" is frequently another way of saying "downscaling the labor force for profit maximization," that workforce "flexibility" is a euphemism for "more easily sackable" and replaceable labor, and that production "flexibility" means a cheapening of labor costs through relocating it offshore (for instance, into "sweatshops"). After all, "speculative and finance capital goes where the labor power is lowest and where the administrative force to guarantee exploitation is highest."[62] What this emerges from is "the immunization of business pursuits against all values other than the maximization of profit," or what Harvey terms the disembedding of capital from a complex web of social and political constraints and interventionist state regulatory activities.[63] Moreover, whereas state governance composed on Hobbesian lines offers protection of the state's citizenry and their private property, the shelter of citizens through welfare systems suffers significant dismantling by being reduced to private power—interests largely untainted by the Keynesian state's interference and public planning. Issues and problems that were formerly public have now become hegemonically reduced to practices conducive only to private responses and solutions. They are so, in fact,

61. Bauman, *Wasted Lives*, 40.
62. Hardt and Negri, *Empire*, 338.
63. Bauman, *Collateral Damage*, 22; Harvey, *A Brief History of Neoliberalism*, 11v.

in ways that enhance the wealth and prestige of those well placed to financially benefit from their provision.

Increasing neofundamentalisms, neonationalisms, and localisms respond by occasionally taking the attractive form of providing depths of meaningfulness.[64] They secure time within the ever-shifting images of a fragmented world, powerful senses of belonging in an era of occupational insecurity, flexible short-termism and necessary "transversal mobility," and stable identities that counter the superficiality of the endless reconstructions of momentary consumerist egos that are fashionably "all dressed up with nowhere to go."[65] Yet these nationally imagined communities, sentimental celebrations of a romanticized locality configured in a territorial politics of purity, miss the irreversible reconfigurations of power in the global economy. "Empire," Hardt and Negri maintain, certainly "cannot be resisted by a project aimed at a limited, local autonomy."[66] In fact, assigning desire to the local serves to distract from the real flows of hegemonically disciplining power, and "obscures and even negates the real alternatives and the potentials for liberation."[67] After all, "there is no outside to the world market: the entire globe is its domain."[68] Furthermore, as Anthony Giddens observes in his 1999 Reith

64. See Robertson, "Glocalization," 176; Bauman, *Collateral Damage*, 65.
65. Citation from Hardt and Negri, *Empire*, 253. See Bauman, *Work*, 27.
66. Hardt and Negri, *Empire*, 206.
67. Hardt and Negri, *Empire*, 46.
68. Hardt and Negri, *Empire*, 190.

Lectures, "Our lives, our personalities, our identities, our emotions, our relationships with other people —these are being reshaped by globalising processes, because globalisation invades local culture. It invades the local context of life and it forces us to live in a more open, reflexive and individualised way."[69] The very idea of "the local," therefore, is a deception if by that is hermetically imagined some purity uninformed and sealed against global networks and currents of power. Finally, and just as alarmingly, relationships assume the terms set by the market's segmentalizing of human identification through a competitive individualism in a regressive ethnicized identity-politics.

The Damage of Not Being Overconsumption

Moreover, fears over the dangers of unsustainable overconsumption have not abated, and for the moment remain a fashionable moral crusade. The idea of "sustainable development," initially articulated in the 1987 report of the World Commission on Environment and Development, *Our Common Future*, is a substantive principle with dramatic normative implications for behavioral adjustment. And yet, globalization, if untempered in the depth of its type of consumptiveness, is not a strategic instrument. This is evident in the fact that, for instance, the inequality

69. Anthony Giddens, *Runaway World: The Reith Lectures Revisited*, The Director's Lectures (November 1999), Lecture 1.

of economic distribution encourages, for example, the Brazilian underclasses to clear and farm the rainforests "as one of their only hopes for economic advancement."[70] It does not invest in the future, but can contribute to what Marx called the "robbing [of] the earth."[71] As a result of its suffused consumerism and its character as "surplus society," it stresses temporary engagements that should not outlast the time required to gluttonously consume the desired objects (or for the desirability of those objects to wane). As George H. W. Bush, when US president, famously announced prior to the Earth Summit in Rio in 1992 (United Nations Conference on Environment and Development), the American standard of living is "not negotiable." That indicates, as Paul Ehrlich maintains, that the problem of depleting resources is not so much one of global population numbers as of the disposability of those resources to an ever-increasing number of consumers. "The impact of humanity on Earth's life support system is not just determined by the number of people alive on the planet. It also depends on how those people behave. When this is considered, an entirely different picture emerges: the main population problem is in wealthy countries. There are, in fact, too many rich people."[72] The point is an important one. "It has wisely been said that the earth can certainly support a popu-

70. Tanner, 120.
71. Karl Marx, *Das Kapital I, Marx-Engels Werke*, vol. 23 (Berlin: Dietz, 1962), 529.
72. Paul Ehrlich, cited in Bauman, *Wasted Lives*, 44.

lation of ten billion people but not ten billion middle-class people."[73]

And yet, despite these tensions and unresolved problems, Fukuyama's claims share the continued use of rhetoric about the inevitability of globalization, couched as observation but operating more at the level of ideology .[74] It evokes an almost eschatological sense about the unpreventability of the universalization of the principles of free market economies.

73. Boyle, *Who Are We Now?*, 117.

74. See, e.g., Thomas L. Friedman, "Quit the Whining: Globalization Isn't a Choice," *International Herald Tribune* (30 September 1997); Bill Clinton, speech to the World Trade Organization, 19 May 1998, cited in Hines, *Localization*, vii; Tony Blair, speech to the World Trade Organization, 19 May 1998, cited in Hines, *Localization*, vii.

3

Practicing Glocalized Religion for Life?

Chapter 2 has taken this book to the point of being concerned about the lack of time for being oneself-as-an-other, to use Paul Ricoeur's image.[1] In this context, theological reflections over the disciplinary conditions for identity construction in a hegemonic globalized capitalist system can learn from concerns over the loss of democratic participation in political

1. Paul Ricoeur, *Oneself as Another*, trans. Kathleen Blamey (Chicago: University of Chicago Press, 1992).

life (such as those of Wendy Brown, Henry Giroux, Zygmunt Bauman, among others) in critiques of neoliberal reconfiguration of values.

What Does "Religion" Publicly Solve?

At this point a cheap apologetic trick could offer a "framework," to adapt Charles Taylor's concept, of a form of resistance as a *solution*—the "only Christianity" type that rhetorically populates a number of responses to sociopolitical critiques of the neoliberal market's reconstrual of time and space.[2] Several years ago, Richard Roberts offered a slightly different type of response. He argued that "religion" could aid the public arena by providing resources for an "emancipatory" hope capable of offering political resistance and visions for change.[3] To cite Ward's critical response to Huntington, "religion may be the hope for the making of a new world order rather than the dry tinder awaiting ignition."[4] Roberts laments the privatization of religion, the vacating of public spaces and the retreat into uncritical and conservative sentimentalities or nostalgic fantasies for ages past. For this reason he launches vibrantly acrimonious, occasionally even

2. See Charles Taylor, *Sources of the Self: The Making of Modern Identity* (Cambridge: Cambridge University Press, 1989).
3. Richard H. Roberts, *Religion, Theology and the Human Sciences* (Cambridge: Cambridge University Press, 2002), citation from 249.
4. Graham Ward, *The Politics of Discipleship: Becoming Postmaterialistic Citizens* (Grand Rapids: Baker Academic, 2009), 144.

acerbic, critiques of Karl Barth and John Milbank for doing just that with what he identifies as their totalitarian voices.[5] It is in a tone of celebration that Roberts announces that "religion returns from the theoretical and cultural periphery (a marginalisation promoted by traditional secularisation theory) into a close relation to the core issues of our time."[6]

Roberts attempts to keep conversation open and global in range without inventing a "common good" with the name of a "global ethic" (Hans Küng) or a "global civilization" (Ninian Smart), and he does so without permitting "religion" to either impose a hegemony on "nonreligious" discourses or to disappear into its time for private consolation or meaning. It may well, at its best, open up traditions to *ad hoc* alliances in resisting systems conducive to the hopelessness that comes from injustice, despair, and the thanatizing-drive.

Whose Globality, Which Religion?

However, Roberts's efforts are themselves not without some difficulty. Although a paper of 1998 suggests that the conditioning of "embodiment" is vitally important to his sensibilities, Roberts criticizes these thinkers not

5. On Roberts's assessment of Milbank, see "Theology and the Social Sciences," in *The Modern Theologians: An Introduction to Theology in the Twentieth Century*, 2nd edition, ed. David F. Ford (Oxford: Blackwell, 1997), 700–719, especially 709–11.
6. Roberts, *Religion, Theology and the Human Sciences*, 250.

from the standpoint of someone conscious of his own traditionedness.[7] Moreover, his detection of certain resources for a countercultural response to the political abuses of globalization, indeed "possibly one of the few remaining means . . . of outflanking globalized and totalizing power," comes from his sense of *religion in a global form*.[8] While keen not to miss points of incommensurability in "religions," he discovers that there is enough commonality to stress that what it can particularly do is offer a means of confronting some of the more extreme fragmentations of postmodernity. "Global religion" represents a crucial tension between universal and particular without, presumably, succumbing to the universalization of what Roberts calls "contemporary orgies of collective tribal power," or to the manipulation of consciousness for its interests.[9] The "evidence of serious, negotiated convergence of concerns" can celebrate "diversity whilst honouring and seeking to articulate universal exigencies" through promoting "identity" as "a self-transcending identity" of "subversive emancipation."[10]

7. See Richard H. Roberts, "The Embodied Trinity," unpublished paper presented at the Society for the Study of Theology (1998).
8. Richard Roberts, in *Theology and Sociology: A Reader*, ed. Robin Gill (London: Cassell, 1996), 474, a section taken from Richard H. Roberts, "Globalised Religion? The 'Parliament of the World's Religions' (Chicago 1993) in Theoretical Perspective," *Journal of Contemporary Religion* 10 (1995): 121–37.
9. Roberts, "Theology and the Social Sciences," 714.
10. Roberts, *Religion, Theology and the Human Sciences*, 268; Roberts, in Gill, *Theology and Sociology*, 478, 714, 715, respectively.

Nonetheless, at worst this may still appeal to those who imagine that something called "religion" can contribute to the making of an equally nebulous "global ethic." What Roberts's proposals lack is an appropriate sense of specificity, and this is no insignificant matter. The phrase "globalized religion" is a tautology, since to speak of "religion" is already to succumb, in a very real sense, to a global nomination of those religious particulars in the cast of the single entity "religion." In other words, any discourse about "religion" will itself be totalizing by reading the various particularities in a way that reduces them to some banal common denominator that loses the sense of the contextualities of speaking, and Procrusteanly becomes selective in choosing the criteria for assessing what counts as religion. John Hick's religious pluralism is a notorious culprit of this, turning out to be, as several critics have noted, a modern mythologization that illegitimately slips from a particularized perspective into a contextless one. The irony is that for all the ethical worry about the imperialist pretensions of religious exclusivisms, as Kenneth Surin observes:

> the pluralist . . . speaks well of the other but never to the other, and indeed cannot do otherwise because there really is no intractable other for the pluralist. Constitutive features of the pluralist position serve to decompose or obscure that radical particularity which is constitutive of the truly other. . . . The inevitable outcome has been a sheer inattentiveness on the part of

> these thinkers to the intricacies and complexities and political configurations which circumscribe their [own] reflections.[11]

Unlike Hick's, though, Roberts's agenda is less that of one seeking to promote interreligious dialogue, even if that be at the expense of unmarking distinguishing expansive particularities, than that of attempting to encourage theologians and the various religious practitioners to engage in public conversation, and a highly critical one at that, with societies that have marginalized and largely silenced their voices in the public domain.

On the one hand, I would not want (at least at this stage) to question Roberts's assessment of the ethically and politically significant commonalities, especially given his hesitancy to speak about these in the context of a hegemonic pluralist hermeneutic that seeks consensus at the metaphysical level. Roberts is not imposing a politics of "the religious." On the other, however, it is worthwhile, if the discussion is not to remain too abstract and therefore still largely unusable, to press for greater attentiveness to the sheer diversity of human experience, and therefore examine more carefully religions' specificities and differences (differences that may even make the word *religion* itself virtu-

11. Kenneth Surin, "A 'Politics of Speech,'" in *Christian Uniqueness Reconsidered: The Myth of a Pluralistic Theology of Religions*, ed. Gavin D'Costa (Maryknoll, NY: Orbis, 1990), 192–212 (200, 202).

ally unusable). Even if one does not want to go so far as to specify in a moment of metanarration the *incommensurability* of the languages, discourses, and narratives that make and sustain people, it is unduly disingenuous to continue to speak of a sharing of values and vision and of a global *religion* as if of a *genus* without doing considerably more demanding "translation" work and conversing. It may be possible, for example, that convergence on a certain theme and/or practice may be justified in immeasurably different ways, and that those ways themselves may lead to serious divergence over another significant theme and/or practice. Consensus is not necessarily either "natural" or to be expected, but *ad hoc* and to be hoped for. For Ward, for example, it is in the negativity of resistance that overlaps and cooperation are most pronounced: "what unites the faithful communities of these different religious traditions is a common enemy—the godlessness of cultures driven by secular ideals, capitalist rapaciousness, decadent levels of wastage, and a hypocrisy that points to the abuse of human rights abroad and closes its eyes to the inadequate provision for the socially vulnerable at home."[12] Appeals to "globalized religion," then, may serve to be unproductive and distract from this contextuality of religious discourse. Each particular religious locality, and even that is a very fluid entity and one that is dialectically related to

12. Ward, *The Politics of Discipleship*, 144.

the global (as with the "world" religions), may provide resources that ask certain questions of the values and practices of globalization.[13]

The Christian "Solution"

Nicholas Boyle takes a different and more specific approach to potentially resistant forms of globality. He observes that "the worldwide church is one of humanity's truly global institutions."[14] Without significant clarification, however, Boyle's claim might for the less attentive reopen possibilities of Christian hegemony and self-assertive forms of public engagement. Can the church be *the* global agent, even if it claims grandly to have reason to advocate for the well-being of all, given the fact that it is simply unrepresentative of the majority of humankind? Moreover, what kind of regulatory impact can the church have when it is itself replete with divisions, as well as multiple perspectives even over issues such those raised in chapters 1 and 2? Boyle wants a global set of politically significant problems to have a global solution. With this, others such as Hardt and Negri agree:

13. Garrett Green: "As cultural anthropologists have shown us, religions are symbolic systems that are implicated in culture in complex and unpredictable ways, not mere systems of thought that can be abstracted from their cultural context" (*Theology, Hermeneutics and Imagination: The Case of Interpretation at the End of Modernity* [Cambridge: Cambridge University Press, 2000], 47).
14. Nicholas Boyle, *2014: How to Survive the Next World Crisis* (London: Continuum, 2010), 166.

> The mobility of populations makes it increasingly difficult to manage national markets (particularly national labor markets) individually. . . . The tendential realization of the world market should destroy any notion that today a country or region could isolate or delink itself from the global networks of power in order to re-create the conditions of the past and develop as the dominant capitalist countries once did. . . . We have to accept that challenge and learn to think globally and act globally. Globalization must be met with a counter-globalization, Empire with a counter-Empire.[15]

Bauman recognizes that not only are the systems that generate the problems global, but the reach of their deathly impact is global as well.

> There are valid reasons to suppose that on a globalized planet, with the plight of everyone everywhere determining the plight of all the others while being determined by them, one can no longer assure and effectively protect democracy "separately": in one country, or even in a few selected countries, as in the case of the European Union. The fate of freedom and democracy in each land is decided and settled on a global stage; and only on that stage can it be defended with a realistic chance of lasting success. . . . Before it finishes its job . . . modernity needs to perform one more task, one that is yet more formidable: to raise human integration to the level of *humanity*, inclusive of the whole population of the planet. However hard and thorny that task may prove

15. Michael Hardt and Antonio Negri, *Empire* (Cambridge, MA: Harvard University Press, 2000), 253, 284, 206.

> to be, it is imperative and urgent, because for a planet of universal interdependency it is, literally, a matter of (shared) life or (joint) death. . . . At some point, therefore, a resurgence of the essential core of the socialist "active utopia"—the principle of collective responsibility and collective insurance against misery and ill fortune—will be indispensable, though this time on the global scale, with *humanity as a whole* as its object. . . . The "social *state*" is no longer viable; only a "social *planet*" can take over the functions that social states tried, with mixed success, to perform. I suspect that the vehicles likely to take us to that "social planet" are not territorially sovereign states, but rather extraterritorial and cosmopolitan non-governmental organizations and associations; those that directly reach to people in need above the heads of and with no interference from the local "sovereign" governments.[16]

Even if the church cannot imagine itself as a solution, a particular Christian account can offer the capacity for critique and transformation for flourishing. After all, even critique is not a neutral task but one that perspectivally takes shape within quite particular ways of construing things, that always stands somewhere and not nowhere. And it is certainly not possible to disembed it, therefore, from constructively imaginative proposals, as Foucault argues.

16. Zygmunt Bauman, *Collateral Damage: Social Inequalities in a Global Age* (Cambridge: Polity, 2011), 23, 25, 26.

> A critique does not consist in saying that things aren't good the way they are. It consists in seeing on what type of assumptions, of familiar notions, of established, unexamined ways of thinking the accepted practices are based. . . . Criticism consists in uncovering that thought and trying to change it: showing that things are not as obvious as people believe, making it so that what is taken for granted is no longer taken for granted. To do criticism is to make harder those acts which are now too easy.[17]

Foucault continues by recognizing that "understood in these terms, criticism (and radical criticism) is utterly indispensable for any transformation."[18] What eventuates might only be a gesture toward a critique and constructive vision for repair, but it is no less significant for being so, and may be all that is liberatingly available in the polyphony of global voices.

In fact, it is precisely this modest direction that Nicholas Lash's proposals regarding "learning to speak again" take by articulating a theological framing that *demands* not only thick self-description, but a self-reflexivity informed by chastening attentiveness to the descriptions of others (even descriptions of us by others) christologically.[19] From a theological account invested in following what he perceives to be the

17. Michel Foucault, *Power: Essential Works of Foucault 1954-1984*, ed. James D. Faubion (New York: New Press, 1994), 436.
18. Foucault, *Power*, 456.
19. Nicholas Lash, *Holiness, Speech and Silence: Reflections on the Question of God* (Aldershot, UK: Ashgate, 2004), 69.

sociopolitical implications of sharing in the hospitality of the God who was in the crucified and risen Christ on the way to Emmaus, comes a refusal to allow free market apologists to speak their truth with the milk of fatalism, wherein those attempting to imagine alternatives drown. As Boyle argues, "We all live in and by the global market and the first duty of the critic is to understand our position and not succumb to delusions."[20] From just such a radically honest or demythologizing appraisal comes a critical refusal to permit life to be shaped by systems of domination, "soft" as those hegemonic systems may well appear to be to most not immediately caught in the path of the juggernaut of the so-called free market, and a refusal to let their advocates in public loose with bureaucratic technique talk that masks the literally demoralized values whose regulation of practices destroy many others' lives.[21] Philip Kenneson argues that "every human life is 'bent' toward something. Every human life is an act of worship. . . . [A]ll human life is bent towards something or someone that defines ultimate worth."[22] Consequently, imagining resistance through practices that demand an apprenticeship in an alternative way of being-in-time can emerge and engage in

20. Nicholas Boyle, *Who Are We Now? Christian Humanism and the Global Market from Hegel to Heaney* (Notre Dame: University of Notre Dame Press, 1998), 81.
21. See Boyle, *Who Are We Now?*, 44.
22. Philip Kenneson, "Gathering: Worship, Imagination, and Formation," in *The Blackwell Companion to Christian Ethics*, ed. Stanley Hauerwas and Samuel Wells (Oxford: Blackwell, 2004), 53–67 (54).

accountably attentive conversation with other visions of the flourishing of all things.

Such an approach is committed to exploring the complex ways in which the training and retraining of judgment as to what is valuable, of discernment regarding what is to be desired, occurs. Critiques that fail to understand the complexity of the schooling of disposition and perspective through habituated practices fail to do at least two things. First, they fail to perceive how cultivation of understanding about the world and oneself within it, moral judgment, emerge informally. Accordingly, Ivan Illich maintains, "Everyone learns to live outside school. . . . Most learning is not the result of instruction. It is rather the result of unhampered participation in a meaningful [or meaning-making] setting."[23] Illich, therefore, criticizes "any attempt to reform the university without attending to the system of which it is an integral part."[24] As early as 1970, Illich warned that the school was "the reproductive organ of a consumer society."[25] Second, they reinvest a problematic confidence in the disjunction of beliefs and practices that function as an individuated politics of pure and unconditioned practices. Judgments of "choice" do not, therefore, properly lend themselves to atomistic description. The choosing person makes judgments, even when done instinctively

23. Ivan Illich, *Deschooling Society* (London: Marion Boyars, 1970), 28, 39. Cf. 72.
24. Illich, *Deschooling Society*, 39.
25. Illich, *Deschooling Society*, 74.

and not through an extended process of practical reasoning, from within certain frameworks of understanding and desiring. Consequently, as Alasdair MacIntyre argues, it is distinctly troubling that a prominent tendency in modernity has been to partition "each human life into a variety of segments, each with its own norms and modes of behaviour," and a "tendency to think atomistically about human action and to analyse complex actions and transactions in terms of simple components."[26] This entails that life and action appear "as nothing but a series of unconnected episodes." What this amounts to , MacIntyre avers, is "a liquidation of the self" since it renders the denarratable decision-making subject unintelligible and socially unidentifiable. Leaning on MacIntyre's critique of the construal of judgment and decision in modernity and his attempts at repair through offering a narrative embeddedness and form of dependence of the ethical agent, Gregory Jones argues constructively that "people *learn* to describe their actions and lives in one way rather than another, and that people *learn* to acquire or exercise the virtues [and vices] ingredient in making wise [or, in the case of vices, unwise] judgments."[27] To be educated, schooled, formed, cultivated, socialized, disciplined by practices embedded in a dif-

26. Alasdair MacIntyre, *After Virtue: A Study in Moral Theory*, 2nd ed. (London: Duckworth, 1985), 204.

27. L. Gregory Jones, *Transformed Judgment: Toward a Trinitarian Account of the Moral Life* (Eugene, OR: Wipf & Stock, 1990), 2.

ferent political logic shapes persons' desires and rational judgments in markedly different ways.

The direction chapter 4 takes, then, follows from asking what a claim such as that articulated by Raymond Plant—that "in the Eucharistic liturgy we are enjoined to seek the common good" beyond any apolitical or politically individuated construal of liturgical action—might mean in learning political practice.[28] This account would, if successful, *gesture* toward a true "glocality," one in which local practices impact substantially upon the operational values of the global market at the levels of both production and consumption for the sake of sustainably flourishing global life. (The word *gesture* here postulates a hesitation lest readers imagine an odd kind of eucharist, one that compresses the eschatological into a *solution* for "the end of history.")

28. Raymond Plant, *Politics, Theology and History* (Cambridge: Cambridge University Press, 2001), 196. On the political origins of the term *leitourgia* see Graham Ward, "A Christian Act: Politics and Liturgical Practice," in *Liturgy, Time, and the Politics of Redemption*, ed. Randi Rashkover and C. C. Pecknold (London: SCM, 2006), 29–49.

4

A Politics for Eucharistic Adventing

The Sacred in the No-Ordinary Ordinary

While governor of Bithynia, Pliny the Younger famously wrote to his emperor around 112 CE for advice about what to do with a suspect group, the Christians. Referring to some sort of food consumption, he declares that they gathered "to take food, but ordinary and harmless food."[1] The reference to "ordinary" can be theologically pressed into highly significant areas concerning the nature of kenosis and sacramentality, the engracedness of all things, and consequently God's self-glorification in and through the ordinary materials of creation, elected and embodied incarnationally. However, Johann-Baptist Metz speaks of Christianity as being constituted in and through a dangerous memory, and it is the theological dangerousness of the eucharistic memory that Pliny, as unschooled observer, with his phenomenological talk of "harmless food" misses.[2]

Long, Gorringe, and Cavanaugh, for instance, all discover in Christian eucharistic traditions resources for *enabling a response* to globalization's pressures, struggles, and trajectories.[3] However, it is important to warn that "theology needs to be wary of its habits of generalising about the Eucharist."[4] In the first place, eucharistic practices are all too often expressions of Christian politics of exclusion. Concrete eucharistic practicing,

1. Cited in J. Stevenson, ed., *A New Eusebius: Documents Illustrating the History of the Church to AD 337*, rev. ed. (London: SPCK, 1987), 19.
2. Cf. Alberto Moreira, "The Dangerous Memory of Jesus Christ in a Post-Traditional Society," in *Faith in a Society of Instant Gratification*, ed. Maureen Junker-Kenny and Miklós Tomka, Concilium (London: SCM, 1994), 39–48.
3. D. Stephen Long, *Divine Economy: Theology and the Market* (London: Routledge, 2000), 235; Timothy Jarvis Gorringe, "Invoking: Globalization and Power," in *The Blackwell Companion to Christian Ethics*, ed. Stanley Hauerwas and Samuel Wells (Oxford: Blackwell, 2004), 346–59; William T. Cavanaugh, "The World in a Wafer: A Geography of the Eucharist as Resistance to Globalization," *Modern Theology* 15 (1999).
4. David Ford, "What Happens in the Eucharist?," *Scottish Journal of Theology* 48 (1995): 359–81 (365). Cf. Stanley Hauerwas and Samuel Wells, "Christian Ethics as Informed Prayer," in *The Blackwell Companion to Christian Ethics*, ed. Stanley Hauerwas and Samuel Wells (Oxford: Blackwell, 2004), 4–12.

with its frequently attendant gender, racial, sexual, and denominational divisions, near idolizations of the *species*, and dematerialized spiritualizations of Christian life, may well suggest little hope for facilitating and resourcing cultural and political responsibilities, and consequently for providing a healthy nonescapist therapy for our current politically significant desires. Around the table/altar is demonstrated painfully that in the church there are still the old divisions of Jew and Greek, male and female, free and slave, and more recently added is that also of straight and queer. As Walter Brueggemann laments, "Even the Eucharist can be made into an occasion of scarcity, as though there were not enough for all. Such scarcity leads to exclusion at the table, even as scarcity leads to exclusion from economic life."[5] Moreover, talk of church in terms of being the alternate polis can be perilously close to stabilizing and reinforcing these pathological patterns of performance. In the second place, eucharistic performances can also be informed by attempts to understand Christian life and practice apolitically in individualized construals of piety. A "shift in our understanding of the eucharist leads to a corresponding shift in our understanding of the society in which we live."[6]

5. Walter Brueggemann, *Journey to the Common Good* (Louisville: Westminster John Knox, 2010), 34.
6. Nicholas Lash, *His Presence in the World* (London: Sheed & Ward, 1968), 152.

Nevertheless, when reread using the shadow of the liturgically influential Pauline text in 1 Corinthians chapter 11, a kind of *Ur*-text of the eucharistic traditions, as a jumping-off-point, the eucharist may indeed indicate something of the shape and dynamic of Christian hope in a context that demythologizes distorted consumptive performance. In fact, as "the sacrament of renewed human community," it may suggest what a disciplining might involve that generates hope for the flourishing of life together.[7]

"On the night when he was betrayed"

Paul opens his recitation with a temporal coordinate, referring to a particular evening. It was "night," and that night was the night Jesus was betrayed. The betrayal reference is important, not merely because of its Gospel allusion to the actions of Judas, but also to those of Peter. Not only did the disciples disappoint Jesus's hopes for them in Gethsemane, but Peter's denial of Jesus is itself a handing over of his commitment to Jesus, a betrayal and apostasy.

Paul, of course, incorporates this notion of ecclesial apostasy in a way that condemns the Corinthian lifestyle, a way of living that, at the assembly's love (agape) feast entails that, in the strongest terms, they are eating and drinking damnation unto themselves through their exclusionary, hierarchical, and therefore

7. Lash, *His Presence in the World*, 162.

uncharitable, feasting. As will be articulated more fully in the discussion later in this chapter, fasting from this type of feasting, from this impoverishment of eucharistic performance, is what Paul calls for.

That which makes the people ekklesia, in Henri de Lubac's famous phrase "the eucharist makes the church," then, encourages a constant suspicion of premature claims to divine presence, representation, and possession, and offers an ek-static reference to the uncontrollable presence of the excessive fullness of transcendent life—the eucharistic people live in the dispossession of properly ordered dependence.[8] Karl Rahner's blunt reminder is that the church "is a Church of sinners." This is an admission that "is itself a piece of the Church's consciousness of her faith."[9] In fact, if anything, as the note of betrayal informs, the ekklesia has to be informed by the event of recognition of, attention to, and prayer against, sin's threats. By rebuking efforts to claim the eschatological presence of God in the presence of the Corinthian ecclesial body, Paul provides an eschatological reservation that entails that, whatever else it does, the eucharist involves a training in refusing to triumphalize Christian existence and performance, and to associating "the good" of the event of divine action in any unqualified

8. Henri de Lubac, *Corpus Mysticum: The Eucharist and he Church in the Middle Ages*, trans. Gemma Simmonds (Notre Dame: University of Notre Dame Press, 2007), 104.

9. Karl Rahner, *Theological Investigations*, 23 volumes (London: Darton, Longman & Todd, 1961–1992), vol. 6, 255.

way with its own activities. Instead, it induces the church to continually seek God's forgiveness in a self-dispossessing mode of humility.

"Until he comes"

The Pauline passage, nevertheless, does not permit the Christian time-telling to sense the night in any straightforwardly dark or agonistically tragic way. The closing reference "until he comes" (1 Cor. 11:26) functions as temporal punctuation and suggests a refiguring of time in its being bordered by events of cross and the Resurrected's consummating return. Everything happens in between or in the midst, so to speak, of this temporal determination, situating the drama of Christian existence as an eschatological temporality. Time, then, cannot be considered as episodically successive, ontologically neutral, and open to the constructions of the will, but as framed as a given that is being given over to the coming of the One in whose promise it lives and moves.

This is the time for hope.[10] But what kind of hope does the Supper nourish? And hope for what? This second temporal coordinate, it could be surmised, casts the reader's gaze back to the Gospel traditions of Jesus's promise of the inexhaustible celebration and sociality of feasting in heavenly banquets. Yet the

10. Cf. Hans Urs von Balthasar, *Mysterium Paschale: The Mystery of Easter*, trans. Aidan Nichols (Edinburgh: T&T Clark, 1990).

Pauline narrative is not so straightforward. Why and how, after all, should we hope for this?

"He took bread and broke it"

Eucharistic debates have frequently concentrated on the status of the Supper's elements in relation to Christ's presence, in abstraction from questions of either the complex "ecology" of how it actually worked and their proper ecclesial location in the eucharistic act, or in terms of the status of presence as the way of proclaiming that there is no God hiding behind the back of the Christ celebrated through sacramental participation. Further, this question has its own location in the fact that, instead, the eucharist first asks us "Who is it Who gifts us this sacrament?" In other words, without necessarily denying that the question of presence is important, something that is often missed in debates over the eucharist is the role of Jesus as perpetual divine Giver and primordial celebrant, the One who is the eventfulness of God (the dynamic of giving) and the hope-*full* responsibility of human being (the human giftedness and giving back in thankful response). Missing this can leave confusion over where salvation may be found. Eberhard Jüngel, following Karl Barth's fear over Roman Catholic sacramentalism, worries that this is exactly what happens in talk of the church as the universal sacrament of salvation.[11] *Sacramentum* in the New Testament, instead, speaks of the prevenient action of God's Self-presentation, enacted and performed graciously for us through creaturely means—i.e., the humanity of Christ. Human activity can only, Jüngel continues, favoring Barth's interpretation, witness to this prevenience of God's personal presence, and liturgically receive these divine benefits, but cannot represent, extend, repeat, or render causally effective his action.[12]

However, the wider notion of sacramentality can be retained, through the ancient notion of the *corpus triforme*, as the complex multiplicity of Christ's mediation.[13] The ekklesia's nature as sacramental *event*-uates as it participates in, analogues, and is spoken through by Christ. This would mean that the assembly is only being ecclesial when it refuses to claim secure possession of grace which is bestowed through it, resists any and every premature identification with the so-called heavenly "church victorious," and lives instead in excession as one acknowledging that the kingdom of God irreducibly overflows the church. It does so in concrete acts of *caritas* (love) that

11. Eberhard Jüngel, *Theological Essays 1*, trans. J. B. Webster (Edinburgh: T&T Clark, 1989), 191.
12. It was for this reason that the Reformers insisted, against the Mass, that the eucharist was not a repetition or representation of the uniquely and historically offered sacrifice of Christ.
13. Hans Urs von Balthasar, *The Glory of the Lord: A Theological Aesthetics*, vol. 1, *Seeing the Form*, trans. Erasmo Leiva-Merikakis (San Francisco: Ignatius, 1982), 529. On this threefold explanation, see Frederick Christian Bauerschmidt, "The Threefold Body: Theology after Suspicion," *Journal for Christian Theological Research* 2 (1997), reprinted http://home.apu.edu/~CTRF/papers/1997_papers/bauerschmidt.html.

participate in, and are judged and determined by the primordiality of Christ, Christ as the primal sacrament of God.[14] In other words, according to Frederick Bauerschmidt, "It is the quality of life of those who are in Christ that manifests—or fails to manifest—the truth of Christ."[15]

The eucharist is the third form of the tri-form body of Christ (and not the extendability of the primary form). It is not merely illustrative of the being of the assembly but is itself constitutive and regulative of it, the conditioning and determining liturgical core. It is disruptive of bodies made simply as disposable containers for souls, and of the escapological form of the mortification of material life, those features that impoverish confession of divine creativity. The ekklesia's existence is irreducibly identified as eucharistic, and so too those who offer *eucharistia*, thanksgiving—hence to be church is to be continually responsively thankful for the irreducible, unpossessable abundance and inexhaustible plenitude of grace given; for its incorporation into the grace that was God's in Christ, the body broken for us while we were yet sinners. In this, the eschatological dimension teases out meanings of eucharistic presence and graciousness that always speak of a certain type of deferral, or presence of absence—that the One presented to the people

14. See Edward Schillebeeckx, *Christ the Sacrament of the Encounter with God* (London: Sheed & Ward, 1963).
15. Bauerschmidt, "The Threefold Body."

is the inexhaustibly unknowable One who is always coming, and therefore the infinitely rich Giver perpetually excessively Self-giving.[16] This is illustrated in the repeatability and diversity of eucharistic enactments, that God's eschatological Self-gift is continually being given in such a way as to resist forms of eschatological evasion of the eventful coming of God's presence in Christ by disposing of the pressure of the eschaton when it is deferred to futurity, an addition and end to our time. Instead, a sensibility of the continued pressure of the resurrected life of the world in the unpossessably excessive presencing of God in Christ is the condition for temporality itself, the macrocosmic significance of its noncompletable *telos* figure in each and every eucharistic performance. Fulfillment eutopically awaits the eschatological consummation, and the assemblies of God live in the presence of expectation, in the trace of the promise, always coming and becoming as church beyond necrophilia. Otherwise the betraying-church floods the world with a presence that does not body forth a witness to Christ, to the Christ who is no incarnated embodiment of God's own life.

16. Hence, Rahner's language of "the total reality of Christ is always present and efficacious" needs to be eschatologically qualified. But there is room, then, for making the Calvinist trinitarian move—to speak of gracious presencing in union with the trinitarian God by the eschatological Spirit through the redemptive Son. It is not quite accurate to use a *merely*, as if speaking of an emptiness, in Calvin's supposedly mere spiritual presence, pushing the christic body to the heavenly regions of "otherness."

"He took bread and broke it"

The liturgical structure of the Pauline text emphasizes this prevenience. The first stage of the action is the action of Christ in anticipation of the "laying down" of his life (itself an act of resistance to the powers' ability to control his life). Even if it is questionable that the Supper was celebrated during the time of the Passover, the characteristics of Jesus's anticipating the Passover are noteworthy—and, of course, he accounts for his coming sufferings in terms of eschatologically vicarious Paschal sacrificiality. The act was itself an act of hope. Indeed, eschatologically it is *the* primary and archetypal act of hope. Jesus's kenotic universalism acting out of hope for the world as its Giver and High Priest entails that there is vicariousness in his hope—his hope in God's plans for the world through him (the "yet not my will but yours" of Gethsemane), his hope that God will be vindicated (his hope for being resurrected), and his hope that the world will come to participate in his sacramentality (his image bearing of the divine).

Such is the context for human performance in the globality of Christ's hopeful presence, in marked contrast to an eschatology informed more by the destructive despair of catastrophisms couched in terms of apocalyptic belief. Because of these re-formed hopes, and the hopeful acts of this primordial Hoper, time has been opened for an extension of his hoping through participation in his activity. He hopes for us (on behalf of us, and in our place)[17] so that we may hope for him (or, have hope in him for him). In other words, he becomes our hope, and he is our hope precisely as the One who has hoped for us (and therein re-created what it is for a human to hope).[18] We are set on the way of becoming what we are in him as we are hopeful with and because of him—concelebrants given something to celebrate and to engage in celebrating with him. In this *Christ*-ian God-centeredness of hope the world's time can be hoped to be transformed from the uniformity of distorted desire, corruption, and violence endemic to it into inexhaustible novelty in sharing the bounteous divine eventfulness.

So, the eucharist, the time of memorially reenacting the past as a continuous contemporaneousness and hoped-for future, judges, reconfigures and reperforms human hope beyond any consumerist commodification of hope or the dislocation of hope in intensified presence. Here there is a marked contrast to Louis Althusser's understanding of practices such as prayer—as being an "ideological intervention" in

17. Hope is distinguished from desire at least in the sense that the former is *other*-oriented while the latter is self-oriented.

18. This means that, theologically speaking, it is inaccurate to hope for eternal "things" or *eschata*. Rather, Christian hope is for the eternal One, or *eschatos*. In this way, then, questions can be asked about theologies that speak of being human as being (radically or otherwise) future-oriented, unless that Future is the radical Future of God in the One in and for whom creation was gifted, and by whom it was reconciled and redeemed. The "future" is no abstract teleological trajectory, or linear temporality.

which people learn to say "Amen," or so be it, to the "reproduction of the relations of production."[19] What it means to hope, why we hope, what/who we hope for, are all given new meanings incarnationally and eucharistically because it is declared that in Christ we are no longer able to live as the people we thought we were. Time is not the time we think we see and experience as the appearance of historical progress or that which ineluctably marches on, slipping away from us, or that which is simply the neutral condition for action measurable by timepieces. It is rather that which is created, reconciled, and redeemed in Christ. This is the time of the truly new, rupturing the intensification of the same, the immanentism of cultural possibilities, in the divine transformation into an advent-full life in the eventful purifying presence-to-be of God. In this regard, as time engraced and refigured from the disruption of sin, it is inappropriate to speak through metaphors that could suggest any form of temporal evasion by eucharistically transformed persons, as Oliver Davies does when claiming that it "shatters the temporality of the world and draws the worshipping community to the threshold of a different kind of time."[20] "The ordinary temporal structure of our lives," Davies problematically continues, "is radically called into question." It is better to say with

19. Louis Althusser, cited in Long, *Divine Economy*, 88.
20. Oliver Davies, *The Creativity of God* (Cambridge: Cambridge University Press, 2004), 148.

Schmemann that this is not another time, different from the one God has patience for in God's redeeming Spirit; this is not another world, different from the one God has created and given to us. It is our same world, *already* perfected in Christ, but *not yet* in us. It is our same world redeemed and restored in which Christ "fills all things with Himself." . . . The church is not a society for escape—corporately or individually—from this world to taste the mystical bliss of eternity. Communion is not a "mystical experience": we drink of the chalice of Christ, and he gave himself for the life of the world.[21]

It is in this context that it is crucial to recognize Paul's use of the eucharistic liturgy to upset the socially stratified Corinthian power-relations. George Hunsinger argues that "it is evident from this passage [of 1 Cor. 11:17–34] that Paul expected the Corinthian celebration of the Lord's Supper to be a countercultural event, because he expected it to manifest the community's new humanity in Christ."[22] So Richard Horsley notes that Paul uses the verb *synerchesthai* ("to come together") on five occasions in this particular text (vv. 17, 18, 20, 33, 34) and nowhere else other than 14:23, 26.[23] "The term had strong connotations of a

21. Alexander Schmemann, *The World as Sacrament* (London: Darton, Longman & Todd, 1966), 51, 53.
22. George Hunsinger, *Conversational Theology: Essays on Ecumenical, Postliberal, and Political Themes, with Special Reference to Karl Barth* (London: Bloomsbury, 2015), 65.
23. Richard A. Horsley, *1 Corinthians* (Nashville: Abingdon, 1998).

people joining together to form a society (as in Aristotle's political theory, *Pol.* 3.4.3; 3.5.10; 3.6.7; 6.5.2), or of factions reunited (e.g., Aelius Aristides, *Or.* 24.49)." The problem with the Corinthian performance, however, was that although they were gathered in the same place they were "anything but together." They were divided (*schismata*, v. 18) into factions (*haireseis*, v. 19).

Hunsinger's reading of the text indicates the culturally familiar hierarchical seating arrangement that appears to inform the Corinthian performance. While there is no scholarly consensus on the nature of the seating and eating plan, it is possible that the host's wealthy guests ate in a different space (the triclinium) from all the others (the atrium?) and even prior to the later arrival of the slaves for whom, consequently, there would have been little left over. The preeminent positions were reserved for those with wealth and status, and the disparities in the banquet were practiced according to this pattern, particularly given that each of the guests were expected to bring their own provisions. Some persons had an abundance whereas others had little, and the former overindulged themselves to the point of drunkenness while the latter went hungry (v. 21). Paul's critical point does not focus on the issue of drunkenness or gluttony as such. Instead, these adjectives function as cyphers to signal a form of indulgence that designates self-serving rather than an appropriate sharing that embodies serving others-as-oneself. The reference may even be indirectly to

Dionysian celebrations. In the context of the eucharistic celebration of the gospel, "The community was sundered by a display of conspicuous consumption at the expense of the poor and needy. . . . Inappropriate cultural norms had triumphed over Christian behaviour. The real purpose of the eucharist was forgotten."[24] The care of others, the "for you-ness" of the eucharistic gospel, in a community bound abundantly to unity in the extravagantly hospitable giving of God in Christ in which there is no scarcity for the needy, has been jeopardized. As verse 17 suggests, it is therefore not the Lord's Supper, the sign of the radical embrace of God of the people delivered from sin that honors the memory of their Lord, that they are participating in, but some other kind of meal in which satiation and scarcity remain the norm for a culture socioeconomically ordered by something other than the economy of the gift of manna from heaven.[25] And this is to profane the Supper and therefore eat unworthily (v. 27), to despise the church of God by humiliating others (v. 22), and to incur the judgment of God's displeasure (vv. 30–31) through which they would be condemned with the world (v. 32). Roy Ciampa and Brian Rosner put the matter too glibly at one point when commenting that the divisions "reflected poorly on Christ and on themselves."[26] It is true that what was being imaged

24. Hunsinger, *Conversational Theology*, 67.
25. See Joseph A. Fitzmyer, *First Corinthians: A New Translation with Introduction and Commentary* (New Haven: Yale University Press, 2008), 434.

was something other than the union of the assembly with Christ, but Paul emphasizes *the contrast* between the performance and that of the Supper's significance. The behavior of the affluent Corinthian Christians, and their self-understanding (since Paul's sarcasm implies they may have regarded themselves as spiritually superior, v. 19), involves a sense of betrayal ("handing over") of the Supper's very tradition ("handing on"). Again Ciampa and Rosner eminently trivialize what is at stake when they surmise that "Paul is dumbfounded by the insensitivity of this behavior."[27] Paul is instead, Hunsinger more adequately observes, "indignant that the rich conform so fully to this world while being transformed so little by Christ."[28] Their gathering on these occasions does not display the for(-others-)givingness of God eucharistically signified in the rightly ordered performance of the Supper, the ground for the making of Christ's mystical body, but exhibits instead the values of a markedly different form of identity.

The performative eucharistic word is inflected by a collective obligation that redesigns what it means to be free to be "human," to be self-*full*, full of Christ beyond any self-*ishness* or self-*lessness* as self-*loss*. In a deeply humanizing performance, persons' "cultural identities are placed under 'eschatological erasure.'"[29] They are

26. Roy E. Ciampa and Brian S. Rosner, *The First Letter to the Corinthians* (Grand Rapids: Eerdmans, 2010), 543.
27. Ciampa and Rosner, *The First Letter to the Corinthians*, 547.
28. Hunsinger, *Conversational Theology*, 71.

placed in, with, and under conditions that make visible accountability for the sake of human flourishing. They are directed away from the cultural impoverishment of values in the fractured commonality of agencies of sheer arbitrary will and free choice. The reduction of persons to disposability, to the instrumentalizing logic of moral calculus or economic bureaucracy and possessive self-interest, is refused. And notions of time and place are reordered, the times and places that both nurture and infect or disorder the development of selves and their consequential instrumentalization of the lives of others as means rather than ends.[30] That all means that responsibility for the well-being of others is *not additional* to eucharistically schooled subjects, but is of its very substance in the form of Christ's response- and responsibility-making self-presenting. In this regard there is something distinctly odd in I. Howard Marshall's claim that "Paul was concerned not simply with the social causes and consequences of the disorders in the church meal but with the theological significance of what was happening."[31] This suggests that "the theological" was a supplemental concern or one alongside that of community fracture rather than

29. Elizabeth Stuart, "Sacramental Flesh," in *Queer Theology: Rethinking the Western Body*, ed. Gerard Loughlin (Oxford: Wiley-Blackwell, 2007), 65–75 (68), citing Malcolm Edwards.
30. Jean-Luc Marion, *God Without Being*, trans. Thomas A. Carlson (Chicago: University of Chicago Press, 1991), 140.
31. I. Howard Marshall, *Last Supper and Lord's Supper* (Carlisle, UK: Paternoster, 1980), 111.

something deeply embedded in a single concern—the fact that the Corinthians' community exclusions embodied a radically different gospel from that imaged in the liturgy of the Supper. It is better to say, then, that "we cannot receive Christ's body and blood in the Holy Supper while neglecting the needs of those for whom he died. . . . [W]hat the Corinthians had failed to see was that they belonged inseparably to one another, that they were committed to one another's care."[32] Privatized religious rituals for materiality-transcending individuals' pacifying pieties amount to the deprivation of the care of others that God in Christ embraces through grace . In contrast, eucharistically schooled disciples act in the world in a way fashioned by the Self-giving material address of God in Christ through whom the Spirit makes into an engraced people in a logic of abundantly hospitable inclusion.[33] As Horsley recounts,

> What most concerned Paul, apparently, was that the assembly of saints in Corinth, in its social relationships, was beginning to resemble the dominant imperial society to which it was supposedly God's alternative. Ideally the assemblies of the movement were more or less egalitarian communities, intended to embody the tight-knit reciprocal relations and communal solidarity of a village community. In Corinth, by contrast with the much smaller cities of Thessalonica or Philippi, the assembly

32. Hunsinger, *Conversational Theology*, 75, 77.
33. This point is made by Schmemann, *The World as Sacrament*, 28.

> was a tiny horizontal association in the midst of an imperial metropolis that was structured hierarchically into patronage networks dominated by the provincial elite.[34]

It is crucial to note with Gordon Fee, then, that "as with the issue of slavery in Philemon, Paul attacks the system indirectly to be sure, but at its very core."[35] In critical response, he lays bare the significance of the Supper for the more proper shape of their discipleship.

Now there is the fullness of cruciform existence that is freely opened, beyond bare immanentism, to Christ's world as vocationally engaged in witnessing to his work of resacramentalizing places that had been vacated for the secular, rematerializing the secular, subverting its capitalistic self-assertion, and refiguring "separated selves" with a tactile addressivity. Challenged are all our *simulacra*, virtual realities, with the *vere res* (true substance/reality) that the world in Christ is engraced as that hoped for.[36] According to Cavanaugh, "To consume the Eucharist is an act of anticonsumption, for here to consume is to be consumed, to be taken up into participation in something larger than the self."[37]

34. Horsley, *1 Corinthians*, 164.
35. Gordon D. Fee, *The First Epistle to the Corinthians*, rev. ed. (Grand Rapids: Eerdmans, 2014), 603.
36. Ludwig Wittgenstein, *On Certainty* (Oxford: Basil Blackwell, 1969), § 239.
37. Cavanaugh, *Being Consumed*, 84.

Performing the eucharist is a hopeful act that speaks of humanity's having been reperformed in Christ, presented back to God with an Amen in him, "the Eucharist of the world."[38] It does not give us anything to consume and dispose of, as in any egoistic subjectivity of worshipful affectivity, a time-for-oneself. Rather this temporally refigured eucharistic self is only truly itself in its responsibility for the flourishing of others, in other words, in time-to-be-with-and-for-others lived out in active hoping for the world, since it was for the world that humanity in Christ gave the time of his life. So Rahner claims that "through our priestly existence, we are sent out to others."[39] Thus there is an important socializing of hope for the world in its embodied existence, concretely embodied sacramentally, that asks serious questions of the increasing social atomization that marks the contemporary capitalist West, of the strategies of domination in contemporary relationalities (patriarchal, political, cultural, and religious imperialisms), and of the eucharistic pietisms that imagine the eucharistic action as primarily ours. Moreover, undone is any possible spiritualized aesthetization of the sacrament, that which was fueled by medieval adorations consequent upon the clerical wrenching of lay contact with the species from the active participation in the communion. According to

38. Schmemann, *The World as Sacrament*, 44. Cf. 33, 41.

39. Karl Rahner, *The Practice of Faith: A Handbook of Contemporary Spirituality*, ed. Karl Lehmann and Albert Raffelt (London: SCM, 1985), 156.

Hans Urs von Balthasar, aesthetics is inseparable from dramatics, the theo-dramatics that calls forth its echo in mission.[40]

Hence, the eucharist makes demands in order to bring others into the performance of *eucharistia* (thanksgiving), and to aid in the feeding of those living within the multiple poverties who are not to become reducible to the theodicy of an economic calculus.[41] It is this socializing of hope, the vision of a new and qualitatively different world, the "necessary improvisations, . . . articulations and practices" in testimony to the *ex*travagance of "God's creative abundance" as lavish *Self*-giving in "the particularising activity of the Holy Spirit," that can be radical in a world plagued by multiple hungers and ir-*respons*-ible satieties.[42] In eucharistic performance in Christ, "the whole creation becomes what it always was to be and yet failed to be."[43]

40. See Aidan Nichols, *No Bloodless Myth: A Guide through Balthasar's Dramatics* (Edinburgh: T&T Clark, 2000), 4.
41. Modern economic theory does not measure values such as quality of life in terms of deep friendships, or fulfilling work; nor does it measure indices of natural wealth such as mature forests, diverse flora and fauna, clean air, clear waters. (See Michael S. Northcott, *The Environment and Christian Ethics* [Cambridge: Cambridge University Press, 1996], 285, citing A. N. Whitehead.)
42. Citation from Ford, "What Happens in the Eucharist?," 365.
43. Schmemann, *The World as Sacrament*, 44.

Conclusion: Time for Feasting and Fasting

We supposedly now live beyond mythologies in a disenchanted universe, fracturing and displacing the collective tales and shared sense of the good that delude us and take us from the *poiesis* of our self-creative moment-to-moment identification and action. Discourse of "choice" and "freedom" supposedly operates in a metaphysically free zone, describing actions that function purely procedurally and that reason instrumentally. Such actions are generated *ex nihilo* in the momentary episode conditioned only by the indeterminacy of the will.

Yet, each choice "is a decision that is coloured by the sort of person I am; the choice is not made by a will operating in the abstract, but by someone who is used to thinking and imagining in a certain way."[1] Of course, what it even means even to speak well of the "I" is no simple matter. Judith Butler, for instance, construes subjectivity in terms of a subjectivation without subjection. The subject is formed within norms that preexist her, and is therefore socialized and dependent in quite significant ways. Even "the very terms by which we give an account, by which we make ourselves intelligible to ourselves and to others, are not of our making. They are social in character, and they establish social norms, a domain of unfreedom and substitutability within which our 'singular' stories are told."[2] Working from Foucault, Butler continues by announcing that "what I can 'be,' quite literally, is constrained in advance by a regime of truth that decides what will and will not be a recognizable form of being."[3] In fact, Foucault declares, the very notion of the individual "I" is a social fiction, a product of a particular set of beliefs about the way the world is. "Do not demand of politics that it restore the 'rights' of the individual, as philosophy has defined them. The individual is the product of power. What is needed is to 'de-individualize' by means of multiplication and displacement, diverse combinations. The group must not be the organic bond uniting

1. Rowan Williams, "Making Moral Decisions," in *The Cambridge Companion to Christian Ethics*, ed. Robin Gill (Cambridge: Cambridge University Press, 2001), 3–15 (4).
2. Judith Butler, *Giving an Account of Oneself* (New York: Fordham University Press, 2005), 21.
3. Butler, *Giving an Account of Oneself*, 22.

hierarchicalized individuals, but a constant generator of de-individualization."[4]

In this sense, then, in conversation with Butler, Athena Athanasiou pronounces that "Being invariably in communities with other forms of life, in social realms of co-implicated and differently embodied bodies, serves in the first place as an unsettling of the fantasy of a self-sufficient human subject."[5] After all, the very story that one cannot tell is the story of one's own emergence, one's coming-to-be. This fact indicates that there is a pronounced means of dependency that socializes the self. However one comes to characterize one's acting any choice, decision, deliberation, or judgment, one's deliberative acting "does not liberate any of us from our formations."[6] "I am not formed once and definitively, but continuously or repeatedly. I am still being formed as I form myself in the here and now. And my own self-formative activity—what some would call 'self-fashioning'—becomes part of that ongoing formative process."[7] Developing the ethics of Levinas, Butler moves to articulate a form of moral responsibility as made response-able by the call of the Other. "The mode of address, far from being a simple rhetorical

4. Michel Foucault, *Power: Essential Works of Foucault 1954-1984*, ed. James D. Faubion (New York: New Press, 1994), 109.
5. Athena Athanasiou, in Judith Butler and Athena Athanasiou, *Dispossession: The Performative in the Political* (Cambridge: Polity, 2013), 37.
6. Judith Butler, *Senses of the Subject* (New York: Fordham University Press, 2015), 6.
7. Butler, *Senses of the Subject*, 6.

technique, enacts the social constitution of ontology. . . . The mode of address enacts the social possibility of a livable existence."[8]

"Globalization" does not refer to a myth as such, what Mary Midgley refers to as "myths we live by."[9] The flow of capital and goods in a so-called free market economy, the instantaneousness of telecommunications systems, and the increasing opportunities for international travel have entailed that the term "global" features significantly in shaping the contemporary "global imagination," and in determining the choices for not only agency but for subjectivity and culture themselves.[10] Yet these are sets of practices with mythic resonance—the technologically driven flows of capital are far from the end of the free market's reach, and therefore what is meant by capital. As Wendy Brown, David Harvey, Henry Giroux, Zygmunt Bauman, Michael Sandel, among others, argue, the latest stage of capital has contributed to something distinctly new—the economization and commodification of all areas of life in the subjection of the subject to marketization (neoliberalism), the new empire. "All societies are factories of meanings. They are more than that, in fact: nothing less than the nurseries of *meaningful life*. Their service is indispensable."[11] The global

8. Butler, *Senses of the Subject*, 177.
9. Mary Midgley, *The Myths We Live By* (London: Routledge, 2003).
10. Nicholas Lash, *Theology for Pilgrims* (London: Darton, Longman & Todd, 2008), 163.
11. Zygmunt Bauman, *The Individualized Society* (Cambridge: Polity, 2001), 2.

economy, which is more significant than merely economic, is now the dominant disciplining system. The values of the market regulate the very means of valuation unrestricted to merely economic matters, enculturatingly producing and disciplining values. And it contributes the conditions for the biopower of governance, reframing habits under a globally saturating flow of power to determine temporality itself. "We are encouraged to become consumers of time, to think of every moment as having a momentary exchange value."[12] The global markets, in substantive ways, regulate the possibilities for selfhood and provide the temporal context for performance. The neoliberal projects, then, involve a radical, because transformative, social therapy that provides conditions for forming practices and the ideological imagination that legitimates them. That is where Midgley's image of "myth" is more limited—social myths or stories are here not required to ground and sustain atomistic forms of subjectivity since the very patterns of technologically driven consumptive intensity enact a divestment of social relations, render precarious anything other than momentary modes of relating to others, and provide a horizon of de-moralized practices of market production and consumption-with-little-care that harden into habits. We are all individuals now! So Bauman

12. Scott Bader-Saye, "Figuring Time: Providence and Politics," in *Liturgy, Time, and the Politics of Redemption*, ed. Randi Rashkover and C. C. Pecknold (London: SCM, 2006), 91–111 (92).

laments that "globalization appears to be much more successful in adding new vigor to intercommunal enmity and strife than in promoting the peaceful coexistence of communities."[13] Even the poor are, when not de-voiced through public apathy, commodifiedly objectified as those whose poverties can be eradicated by numbers, by the balance of general economic growths elsewhere, or as simply unfortunate losers in an otherwise fairly operating competitive market system. The indications are, therefore, that "modern economic arrangements work against the cultivation of virtue."[14] The globalization of the consumptive self provides conditions that cannot end poverties or deliver time for maximal living without significant global political will. As Bauman laments, precisely the "one thing which has thus far escaped globalization is our collective ability to act globally."[15] If global institutions' operations, actions, plans, and so on, are not made accountable, *morally accountable*, to truly global checks and balances, the dark underside of the times will storm on unabated and systems and institutions of democratic responsibility will continue either to slip away docilely in the new empire or be crushed by cap-

13. Zygmunt Bauman, *Liquid Modernity* (Cambridge: Polity, 2000), 192.
14. D. Stephen Long, *Divine Economy: Theology and the Market* (London: Routledge, 2000), 6.
15. Zygmunt Bauman, "Whatever happened to compassion?," in *The Moral Universe*, ed. T. Bentley and D. S. Jones (London: Demos, 2001), 41–46 (42). Cf. Nicholas Boyle, *2014: How to Survive the Next World Crisis* (London: Continuum, 2010), 35, 150.

ital's global hegemony. The very flourishing of humankind and of the sustaining nonhuman environment is at stake.

As such, globalization does not have the capacity for creating hope beyond the commodified hopes for perpetual instances of instantaneities of self-gratification. It is little wonder that hope appears in short supply. The mood of contemporary Western society in particular is shaped by a determinative political ontology that is conflictual and agonistic. The paths trodden in the past are being identified as the illusory golden pathways that lead nowhere, and certainly not to the hoped-for goal of human progress. Such hoped-for teleology has become perceived as a dangerous fiction and illusion, drawing its imaginative inspiration from the needs and desires of a small section of the race of beings that desperately searches for a means of not facing up to its lostness in a journey from nowhere to nowhere. The naïve optimism generated by the progress ideal, particularly prominent in the late nineteenth century, has been shattered by the global scale of the events of the twentieth century. Without nostalgically and naïvely longing for bygone eras, George Steiner summarizes this mood:

> [The twentieth] century has witnessed a carnival of bestiality. It is the century of the death-camps and the "killing-fields," of a systematic attempt to torture by political regimes and societies of diverse persuasions. Ours is an era of mass-starvation, deportation and the

> taking of hostages. The feasibility of thermo-nuclear and of biological warfare, the laying waste of the planet, mean that the eventuality of human self-slaughter and of ecological finality are no longer macabre fascinations. The autumn and winter of 1989 have brought unexpected, almost miraculous daylight to parts of central and eastern Europe. The air freshens. But prior to its dawning, and throughout much of the rest of mankind, Kafka's stark finding that "there is abundance of hope but none for us" may prove to be sober reportage.[16]

According to Steiner, an overwhelming pessimism can be the outcome for consciousness of "the dark silence of God's absence."[17] Or as David Bell argues, with reference to the macabre journeying of this century's history, "the world . . . holds absolutely no consolation for human beings."[18] Preeminent expression of this may be discovered in the existence of cultures that have been starved and beaten of all hope and imagination of the future. However, such bleakness cannot be endured easily, as Steiner argues in respect of "absolute tragedy."[19]

In this context the culture of the "free play of *différance*" and the celebration of the "carnival" appears

16. George Steiner, "Absolute Tragedy," in *No Passion Spent: Essays 1978-1996* (London: Faber & Faber, 1996), 129–41 (134).
17. George Steiner, *Language and Silence: Essays 1958-1966* (Harmondsworth, UK: Penguin, 1969), 204.
18. David F. Bell, "Introduction: Of Silence and Insouciance in Philosophy," in Clément Rosset, *Joyful Cruelty: Towards a Philosophy of the Real*, trans. David F. Bell (Oxford: Oxford University Press, 1993), vii–xvi (viii).
19. Steiner, "Absolute Tragedy," 129.

to largely be a laughing in the face of despair, the staving off of the anxiety of being adrift in a postmodern, post-death-of-God world.[20] Ulrich Beck's comment appears pertinent: "Where there is no escape, people ultimately no longer want to think about it" (hence the hedonistic escapism of "drug-cultures").[21] Escape comes primarily through apathy, or suicide. One needs some form of light to dispel this darkness, for in the dark the demons strike. A not wanting to "think the worst" occurs with those who refuse to learn the lesson of needing to look into the void. In certain quarters the song may still be heard that science and technology offer increasing possibilities for control (over self, society, etc.), particularly in relation to the future. Francis Fukuyama, for example, according to Nicholas Lash, "supposes there to be no thinkable alternative to an historicist understanding of history as a tale of progress, an 'evolution from primitive to modern.'"[22] Similar rhetorically masked ideological forms of lighting the way into the future appear in forms of what is known as "religious fundamentalism." The way of fundamentalism—an aggressive nostalgia—is a boarding of a ship of fools in order to escape the land-based

20. Jacques Derrida, *Margins of Philosophy*, trans. Alan Bass (Chicago: University of Chicago Press, 1982), 27; Kenneth Gergen, *The Saturated Self: Dilemmas of Identity in Contemporary Life* (New York: Basic Books, 1991), 189.
21. Ulrich Beck, *Risk Society: Towards a New Modernity* (London: Sage, 1992), 37.
22. Nicholas Lash, "Beyond the End of History?," *Concilium* 5 (1994): 47–56 (47), citing Francis Fukuyama, "The End of History?," *The National Interest* 16 (1989): 18, and "A Reply to My Critics," *The National Interest* 18 (1989–90): 23.

demons named "legion," never venturing beyond the assumed tranquil waters of its immediate location. David Tracy describes this fundamentalism: "The very violence of the fundamentalist rejection of modernity illuminates the desperation of human subjects sensing their loss of all community, tradition, and values as they feel the terror of a history become empty and meaningless."[23]

Nicholas Boyle argues that "we all make up one world, even if we are only gradually coming to recognize it."[24] The question of what hope might look like in that context is a pressing one. Bauman declares that "the question is not how to turn back the river of history but how to fight against its pollution by human misery and how to channel its flow to achieve a more equitable distribution of the benefits it carries."[25] Michael Northcott, to some degree, echoes this sentiment: "We cannot wish this globality away. But we can challenge its deleterious effects on the poor of the world, and on their degraded environments."[26] In one sense, however, Northcott's comments may actually appear to be insufficiently radical. What is worth critical attention is not "globality" as such, but the "pow-

23. David Tracy, "On Naming the Present," Concilium 1990/1 (London: SCM, 1990), 66–85 (74).
24. Nicholas Boyle, *Who Are We Now? Christian Humanism and the Global Market from Hegel to Heaney* (Edinburgh: T&T Clark, 1998), 9.
25. Zygmunt Bauman, *Does Ethics Have a Chance in a World of Consumers?* (Cambridge, MA: Harvard University Press, 2008), 75.
26. Michael S. Northcott, *The Environment and Christian Ethics* (Cambridge: Cambridge University Press, 1996), 326.

erful systems of formation" for human identity in a globalized world, systems that found and discursively ground the various socioeconomic and cultural problems in the contemporary world.[27] In this respect, then, the economics of the global market cannot be culturally referred to without "globalism," or cultural "one-worldism," what Martin Albrow names the "global society."[28] Moreover, the rhetoric that speaks of the global economy without reference to policy decisions and practices of agents, but mystifies economic processes in terms of suggesting some irresistibly runaway world, is to be resisted and exposed.[29] As Leonidas Donskis laments, "The world has probably never been so inundated with fatalistic and deterministic beliefs as it is today. . . . In this widespread atmosphere of fear and fatalism, the conviction arises that there are no alternatives to contemporary political logic and to the tyranny of the economy or to attitudes towards science and technology and the relationship

27. William T. Cavanaugh, *Being Consumed: Economics and Christian Desire* (Grand Rapids: Eerdmans, 2008), 47.

28. Martin Albrow, "Globalization, Knowledge and Society," in *Globalization, Knowledge and Society*, ed. M. Albrow and E. King (London: Sage, 1990). Cf. David Held, introduction to *A Globalizing World? Culture, Economics, Politics*, ed. David Held (London: Routledge, 2000), 1–4 (2).

29. Tony Schirato and Jen Web indicate the need for a genealogy that can trace the noninevitability of the global neoliberal project (*Understanding Globalization* [London: Sage, 2003], 27). Cf. Manfred B. Steger, *Globalization: A Very Short Introduction* (Oxford: Oxford University Press, 2003), 100; Julie A. Nelson, "Breaking the Dynamic of Control: A Feminist Approach to Economic Ethics," *Journal of Feminist Studies in Religion* 19 (2003): 33, cited in Marion Grau, *Of Divine Economy: Refinancing Redemption* (London: T&T Clark, 2004), 1.

between nature and humanity."[30] Yet, "The triumph of rampant, individual and individualizing consumerism over the 'moral economy' and social solidarity was not a foregone conclusion. A society pulverized into solitary individuals and (crumbling) families could not have been built without Thatcher first thoroughly clearing the building site."[31]

Cavanaugh speaks of the eucharist as providing "resistance" to these cultural-economic productions, and one should add, a refusal to reduce the complex multiple manifestations of poverty to simple economic terms. He even goes as far as acclaiming the "Eucharist as antidote to globalism."[32] After all, "The eucharist is unique as being the structural focus of the life of the community, as being that act from which all her other acts, sacramental and otherwise, draw their meaning and efficacy."[33] The problem, however, is that concrete eucharistic performances, in all their failures to be peacemaking, bare the impress of the night of betrayal, the night that also scapegoated Judas, and perhaps impressing the image of Judas as a type on the Jewish people as a whole, thereby betraying the for(-others-)givingness of God in eschatological embrace. Churches are themselves inadvertently caught up in pressures

30. Leonidas Donskis, in Zygmunt Bauman and Leonidas Donskis, *Liquid Evil* (Cambridge: Polity, 2016), 1.
31. Zygmunt Bauman, *Consuming Life* (Cambridge: Polity, 2007), 145.
32. William T. Cavanaugh, *Theopolitical Imagination: Christian Practices of Space and Time* (London: T&T Clark, 2003), 116.
33. Nicholas Lash, *His Presence in the World* (London: Sheed & Ward, 1968), 56.

of wider cultures, and in the unseen motors of those darknesses. Consequently, Cavanaugh admits, "many of our Eucharistic celebrations . . . have been colonized by a banal consumerism and global sentimentality. The logic of globalization infects the liturgical life of the Church itself: Christ is betrayed again at every Eucharist."[34]

Yet the liturgy of the eucharistic performance speaks not only of liturgical formation but also of *trans*formation. A certain account of the eucharist can argue that what it, as ritualized and performed "word," can do is speak of, and therein reperform when it is heard, time's having been opened eschatologically. It can both fashion and demand the polis-fashioning of a form of subjectivity/selfhood that is preeminently hopeful in the incessant dynamic of learning-to-be in many ways of relating to others that are economically, politically, and culturally responsible.[35] The utilitarian calculations of market processes are refused their ontological nihilisms. Our time is not free to be kept from others as if it is time for us to eat-for-ourselves, because God has given time for creation through a form of consuming that feeds others, so that creation's time may be incessantly *eucharistia*, thankfulness, to God. This is less a matter of "you are what you eat" as "you are with whom you eat."

34. Cavanaugh, *Theopolitical Imagination*, 121.

35. This is a reading that contests Hayek's account of Christianity's "basic individualism" to "shape their own life" (cited in Long, *Divine Economy*, 105).

Therein it is given that God in Christ still has time for creation because God still has hope for it. There is here a refusal to let any part of the darknesses of that creation remain unhoped for, or be feared, even the night's "witching hour." The Christian theologian, at least, is bound to hope, and that hope, to use Terry Eagleton's language, is "a species of permanent revolution."[36] By the Spirit of Christ she is taken up into the life-giving promise of the renewal of all things in Christ. Despair, for instance, over the seeming inexorability of the progress of globalist consumer culture is here denied any ultimacy, as consumerism's contingency is unmasked. The watchful waiting that is commanded of the church is the strange kind of waiting that hopes by its own fragile and tentative, but nonetheless risked, acts of hope. These acts, if they are truly full of Christian hope, participate in the healing en*light*ening of the world by the One who darkly bears the scars until the end of that world.

The direction that that agency may take may not yet be blueprint-able. However, interrogating, in Lash's terms, "all *un*relationship, *un*brotherhood, all domination and division," may be a good ascetic place to start, eucharistically.[37] This will involve what Raymond Williams calls the "unlearning" of "the inherent domi-

36. Terry Eagleton, *Hope Without Optimism* (Charlottesville: University of Virginia Press, 2015), 69.

37. Nicholas Lash, "Conversation in Gethsemane," in *Radical Pluralism and Truth: David Tracy and the Hermeneutics of Religion*, ed. W. Jeanrond and J. Rike (New York: Crossroad, 1991), 56–61 (57).

native mode."[38] In doing this, one may find that globalization's consumerist underpinnings fare badly in the examination. After all, John Kavanaugh's and Timothy Gorringe's point is that the problem is one of "idolatry."[39] Accordingly, a new community of responsible consumers who do not reduce I-You and I-It relations to the self-interested logic of instrumental reason and the commodity form of the competitive marketplace must emerge and flourish in the gift of life abundant that is given for all God's creatures.

This multilocal transformation of temporal *understanding* remains very far from providing effective forms of global resistance to the hegemonic commodification system. Foucault accordingly warns, albeit with too rhetorically overblown a separation of beliefs and practices, that "the problem is not changing people's consciousnesses—or what's in their heads—but the political, economic, institutional regime of the production of truth."[40] Theologians would do well not to invest their rhetoric with grand optimistic-sounding claims but to practice a eucharistically chastened and reconfigured temporal literacy that reads time as the context of giving, embracive for-giveness, and

38. Raymond Williams, *Culture and Society, 1780-1950* (London: Chatto & Windus, 1958), 376.

39. John Francis Kavanaugh, *Following Christ in a Consumer Society: The Spiritualty of Cultural Resistance* (Maryknoll, NY: Orbis, 1981), viii, 11; Timothy J. Gorringe, *Capital and the Kingdom: Theological Ethics and Economic Order* (Maryknoll, NY: Orbis, 1994), viii.

40. Foucault, *Power*, 133.

therefore terra-forming or altern-ing or mondializing hope. Such a performance would embody a hopeful witness, as a performative glimpse and foretaste, to the eucharistic figuration and transformative reconfiguration of all things, enacting a "therapy of desire" in the eschatological good of God in Christ hospitably renewing all things for their proper shared flourishing together.[41]

41. Daniel M. Bell Jr., *Liberation Theology After the End of History: The Refusal to Cease Suffering* (London: Routledge, 2001), 4.

Select Bibliography

Bauman, Zygmunt. *Collateral Damage: Social Inequalities in a Global Age*. Cambridge: Polity, 2011.

———. *Consuming Life*. Cambridge: Polity, 2007.

———. *Strangers at Our Door*. Cambridge: Polity, 2016.

———, and Leonidas Donskis. *Moral Blindness: The Loss of Sensitivity in Liquid Modernity*. Cambridge: Polity, 2013.

Bell, Daniel M., Jr. *The Economy of Desire: Christianity and Capitalism in a Postmodern World*. Grand Rapids: Baker, 2012.

Boyle, Nicholas. *2014: How to Survive the Next World Crisis*. London: Continuum, 2010.

Brown, Wendy. *Undoing the Demos: Neoliberalism's Stealth Revolution*. New York: Zone Books, 2015.

Butler, Judith. *Notes Toward a Performative Theory of Assembly*. Cambridge, MA: Harvard University Press, 2015.

Castells, Manuel. *The Rise of the Network Society*, 2nd ed. Oxford: Blackwell, 2000.

Cavanaugh, William T. *Field Hospital: The Church's Engagement with a Wounded World*. Grand Rapids: Eerdmans, 2016.

Friedman, Milton. *Capitalism and Freedom*. Chicago: University of Chicago Press, 1962.

Fukuyama, Francis. *The End of History and the Last Man*. New York: Free Press, 2006.

Giddens, Anthony. *How Globalization Is Re-shaping Our Lives*. London: Profile Books, 1999.

Giroux, Henry A. *Dangerous Thinking in the Age of the New Authoritarianism*. London: Routledge, 2015.

Hardt, Michael, and Antonio Negri. *Empire*. Cambridge, MA: Harvard University Press, 2000.

Harvey, David. *A Brief History of Neoliberalism*. Oxford: Oxford University Press, 2005.

Long, D. Stephen. *Divine Economy: Theology and the Market*. London: Routledge, 2000.

Miller, Vincent J. *Consuming Religion: Christian Faith and Practice in a Consumer Culture*. New York: Continuum, 2005.

Polanyi, Karl. *The Great Transformation*. Boston: Beacon, 1957.

Rieger, Joerg. *No Rising Tide: Theology, Economics, and the Future*. Minneapolis: Fortress Press, 2009.

Sandel, Michael. *What Money Can't Buy: The Moral Limits of Markets*. London: Allen Lane, 2012.

Žižek, Slavoj. *Against the Double Blackmail: Refugees, Terror and Other Troubles with the Neighbours*. London: Allen Lane, 2016.

Index